Todd Solondz

Contemporary Film Directors

Edited by Justus Nieland and Jennifer Fay

The Contemporary Film Directors series provides concise, well-written introductions to directors from around the world and from every level of the film industry. Its chief aims are to broaden our awareness of important artists, to give serious critical attention to their work, and to illustrate the variety and vitality of contemporary cinema. Contributors to the series include an array of internationally respected critics and academics. Each volume contains an incisive critical commentary, an informative interview with the director, and a detailed filmography.

A list of books in the series appears at the end of this book.

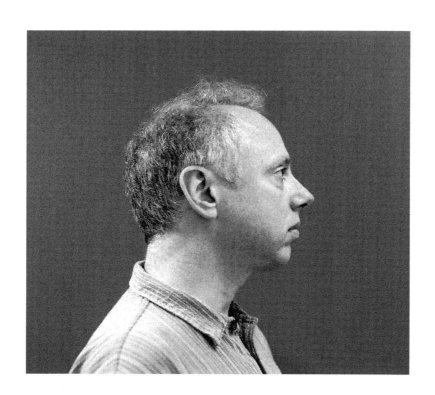

Todd Solondz

Julian Murphet

**UNIVERSITY
OF
ILLINOIS
PRESS**
URBANA,
CHICAGO,
AND
SPRINGFIELD

© 2019 by the Board of Trustees
of the University of Illinois
All rights reserved
1 2 3 4 5 C P 5 4 3 2 1

♾ This book is printed on acid-free paper.

Frontispiece: Todd Solondz. Photograph by Tanya Posternak.

Library of Congress Cataloging-in-Publication Data
Names: Murphet, Julian, author.
Title: Todd Solondz / Julian Murphet.
Description: Urbana : University of Illinois Press, 2019. | Series: Contemporary
    film directors | Includes bibliographical references and index. | Includes
    filmography. |
Identifiers: LCCN 2019006662 (print) | LCCN 2019008968 (ebook) |
    ISBN 9780252051623 (e-book) | ISBN 9780252042768 (hardcover : alk. paper) |
    ISBN 9780252084591 (pbk. : alk. paper)
Subjects: LCSH: Solondz, Todd—Criticism and interpretation.
Classification: LCC PN1998.3.S598 (ebook) | LCC PN1998.3.S598 M87 2019 (print)
    | DDC 791.4302/33092—dc23
LC record available at https://lccn.loc.gov/2019006662

Contents

Acknowledgments	ix
THE LAW OF DIMINISHING RETURNS	1
Non-Place and How to Live There	8
Left Classicism	25
Eternally Diminishing Returns	52
Screens of Fantasy, Durations of the Real	92
The Gift of Shit	110
AN INTERVIEW WITH TODD SOLONDZ	139
Filmography	163
Bibliography	171
Index	173

Acknowledgments |

Justus Nieland and Jennifer Fay, whom I have had the great pleasure to meet, were the deciding factors in bringing this book to print. Their enthusiasm for the project and their constant support, from the moment I first floated it with them, have been tremendously encouraging. It is wonderful to see a series such as this important one in their capacious and expert hands. Daniel Nasset has been a constant boon, always reliable, punctual, and generous. In fact, the entire experience of working with the University of Illinois Press has been consistently positive.

My colleagues at the School of the Arts and Media at UNSW Sydney have been supportive. I'd particularly like to thank the wisdom and advice of George Kouvaros, Jodi Brooks, Alexander Howard, and Jane Mills.

I first studied Todd Solondz for a lecture series at the University of Sydney, which I delivered with Kate Lilley and Melissa Hardie, both of whom are true cognoscenti of the oeuvre. A group of students who saw that lecture (which may have gone down in legend—not least for the moment at which the source sound failed during a screening of the scene where Allen details his fantasies about Lara Flynn Boyle, and I immediately proceeded to overdub the monologue from memory) has stayed in the orbit of that unsettling masterpiece *Happiness*. Solondz has been an inspiriting force for some of the most talented young people I've been privileged to know: Mark Steven, Stefan Solomon, Sam Dickson, and Mark Azzopardi.

I cannot say how grateful and indebted I am to Todd Solondz himself, who has been extraordinarily generous with his time, as interviewee, correspondent, and editor (of the interview, at least). I had few doubts in advance that his was a sensibility and intelligence I would savor, but nothing could have prepared me for his kindness and warmth. Speaking with him about his work for over two hours was one of the great pleasures of my working life.

I first saw *Happiness* with my father, Richard Murphet, who was visiting me in Oxford at the time, prior to a trip we made together to the Low Countries of northwestern Europe, where he was touring his amazing work. This provides me with an occasion to thank him, profoundly, for the extraordinary education in film that he, as a part-time parent, was able to give me—in repertory cinemas of New York in the summer of 1979; in the amazing collection of VHS cassettes he amassed over decades (and the DVD library since); and here, there, and everywhere over the years, stepping into cinemas with me and my sons to watch the extraordinary, the unexpected, and the bizarre. Our afternoon with Solondz in 1998 ranks as one of the most remarkable.

The time spent writing this book was vastly improved by the companionship and affection of the lovely Tamlyn Avery, who braved the home screenings of this filmmaker's body of work. We may have lost her in the final moments of *Wiener-Dog*, Todd, but that she shares a basic worldview with your disabused satire was never in question. For putting up with me, Tam, a million kisses.

Todd Solondz |

The Law of Diminishing Returns |

"I always presume every movie I make is my last," Todd Solondz wryly tells an interviewer. "My career is very smoothly in decline, each movie making half as much as the prior one."[1] A commentator concurs: "Since Todd Solondz's breakout second feature *Welcome to the Dollhouse* (1995) grossed nearly $4.8 million, the trajectory of his career has been decidedly downward, with each new film grossing half of the previous box office, culminating in *Palindromes* (2004), which promptly put his once promising career in limbo."[2] A graph of the fortunes of the box-office grosses across his twenty-year oeuvre all but confirms this estimate (see chart 1).

With two insignificant exceptions, the picture is one of a wholesale decline in fortunes, which can perhaps be amplified, or at least thrown into evaluative relief, by a chart of the aggregate ratings of his films on *Rotten Tomatoes* (see chart 2).

While the critics have rallied to his defense after their inexplicable dismissal of *Palindromes*, reviewers from the Rotten Tomatoes film re-

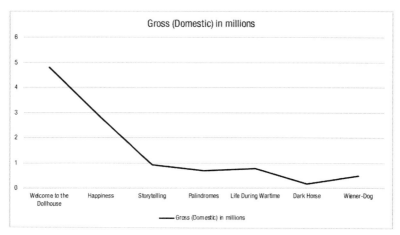

Chart 1. Gross (domestic) in millions of dollars for Solondz films

view website have only doubled down on their rejection of the Solondz brand, with his last three films failing even to score a pass. Solondz himself has a rational explanation for this sorry tale of shrinking returns.

> It's never been easy to get money for films outside the studio system; it's always been very, very difficult. But I think now the difficulties have moved into another phase, where I don't think there's any going back. . . . The market has redefined what makes economic sense and what is possible for a filmmaker outside of the studio system. . . . Movies continue to get made and I think will continue to get made, and I think there will continue to be very impressive and surprising work to come—however, there is much less money to invest in these films. So what might once have been, say, a two-million-dollar movie ten years ago will now have a budget, let's say, of one point two. There's just less money. So you have to rethink and reconceive your ideas for movies so that they are viable. The reasons, I think, are clear to most people. The market, the audience has shrunk because, of course, the Internet, the Netflix, the streaming, the downloading, the pirating, the cable TV with a thousand channels. It makes it difficult to convince people to go out of the home, to spend money as a rival to what they already have at home. The studio movies seem to still be thriving, nevertheless, because

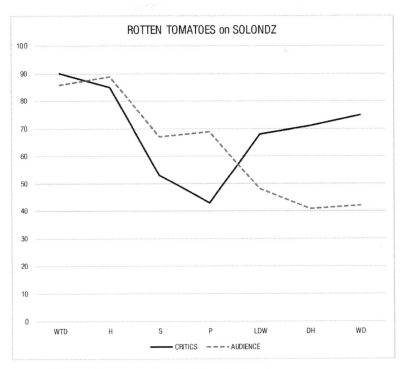

Chart 2. Rotten Tomatoes ratings for Solondz films
(WTD: *Welcome to the Dollhouse*; H: *Happiness*;
S: *Storytelling*; P: *Palindromes*; LDW: *Life During
Wartime*; DH: *Dark Horse*; WD: *Wiener-Dog*)

of the way in which they are able to market and exploit their product, but that's not something that's accessible to the non-studio filmmaker.[3]

As a writer-director with a declared lack of interest in directing other people's work, or in writing more obviously commercial fare, Solondz has self-consciously boxed himself into a corner where the competition for his natural audience share (educated urbanites of a certain age, class, and color) is fierce, technologically driven, and diversifying. Rather than bend to the market and adapt to its changing ecology, Solondz has stubbornly preferred to test the appetite among investors for exactly what it is he has always offered: a cinema of abrasive satirical perceptions and

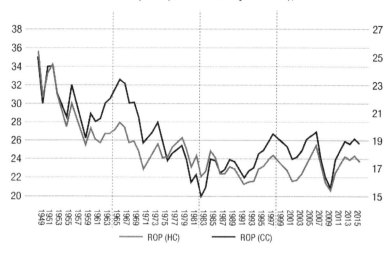

Chart 3. The US rate of profit, 1949–2015 (Source: Michael Roberts Blog, October 4, 2016)

an unyielding style, whose mordant commentaries on American social conditions offer little enough in the way of extenuation or apology, let alone affirmation.

As it turns out, however, the precipitous decline in Solondz's fortunes is an accentuated mirror for the decline in American profitability more generally. Economist Michael Roberts plots the decline of the rate of profit in the world's most powerful nation in chart 3.

"So between 1948 and 2015," explains Roberts, "the US rate of profit declined between 25–33% depending on whether you measure fixed assets in historic (HC) [or] current costs (CC)."[4] The sharp uptick immediately after the global financial crisis (GFC) in 2008 was already in retreat in 2015. The historical conditions that vouchsafed the USA's soaring profitability after World War II—full employment, widespread unionization, state-subsidized public works, aerospace—have been all but obliterated, and the specific physiognomy of free-market capitalism that it exported to the vulnerable parts of the planet—neoliberalism, as it is sometimes called—is facing an unprecedented legitimation crisis. With it becoming increasingly difficult to engineer profits in the US economy over the last three decades, capitalists have tended either to displace production to cheaper labor pools in the developing world, to divert their speculative energies into finance, or to seek "technological fixes" to their balance sheets—typically automation and computerization—in a doomed effort to offset this declining rate of profit. Hammering down wages at home, and fostering a waxing, if stagnant, service sector, postindustrial US capital squeezed a brief windfall of riches before succumbing inevitably to the fact that without rising wages, the internal market for the goods produced was hobbled from the start.

> The social surplus accompanying accumulation has dwindled, and with it the capacity of capital and state to meet demands for both direct and social wages. . . . Capital has shifted its hopes for profit into the space of circulation, and thus shifted its vulnerability there, labor has shifted into circulation with it. So has non-labor: the under- and unemployed, those left to informal economies, those left to molder.[5]

The American decline is starkly visible in its crumbling infrastructure; its expanding rust belts; its "surplus population" living under makeshift and impermanent shelter; its empty, foreclosed housing stock; its disenfranchised ghettoes; and its soaring prison population of black and brown people. But everywhere, in different modalities, the same critical decline can be felt, at levels of diffraction that split into distinct affective spectra and modes of psychic intensification.

The cinema of Todd Solondz presents one such pattern of diffraction, where decline articulates with the relatively protected Lebenswelt of the suburban middle class—with its rare glimpses up into the inaccessible enclaves of the gated rich and its more frequent evacuations into the spatial precariousness of the working poor. In devising a cinema for the messy edges of this "silent majority," Solondz models an ongoing homology between a body of work seemingly intent on belittling its own market share and a national economy unable to deliver sustainable returns to its panicked investors. In this spiraling double helix of decline, we also discern a map of the DNA of contemporary American cinema itself, whose overriding principle is that of the law of diminishing returns. While capital continues to be invested in the motion picture industry, it does so preponderantly at the tech-heavy end of the business, where innovative computer-generated imagery (CGI), home streaming, virtual reality, and gaming tie-ins offer sufficient opportunities for substantial returns, and where large, horizontally integrated production units guarantee a degree of oversight and control. Yet, with an inevitable logic, any enthusiastic investment levels off, as franchises like Marvel's and DC's comic book universes, the *Star Wars* cycle, or the Middle Earth saga, whose potential for long-term dividends diminishes with each installment, exhaust the market, and the crisis is reinitiated. Hollywood, that is to say, makes some money but not the way it used to. Since 1990 the average domestic rate of return, even on successful big-budget productions, has slumped from a budget-to-gross ratio of 2.3:1 to one of 1.2:1 (a figure that omits innumerable "failures" and flops altogether).[6]

Solondz's cinema is an objective correlative of the underlying rule of the capitalist film industry today: unable on the whole to do anything but lose money yet driven to lay increasingly risky bets on the next new thing that, as a rule, is but a variation on the good old things that once upon a time delivered a return of 600 percent—which is exactly the rate of profitability enjoyed by Solondz's breakout (and only) commercial success, *Welcome to the Dollhouse*. The law of diminishing returns that this cycle of films both depicts and enacts is the law of the cinema itself in the age of its coming obsolescence under the digital hegemon. At the same time, these films unsparingly take the temperature of the larger economy, so trapped in a downward spiral of the falling rate of profit that it is unwilling to invest in the material aspects (infrastructure, institutions of public welfare, sustainable communities) that might make profit possible once more. Failure's "centrality to [Solondz's] artistic practice" is thus a powerful hermeneutic.[7] His cinema, I want to say, tells a cumulative story about *value* itself under late capitalism that is very difficult to hear articulated elsewhere in the assorted critical products of the culture industries—namely, that value today is only the ghost of exchange value and that therefore the pursuit of it is, in that sense and others, quite pointless.

As this book argues over a number of interrelated themes and topics, it is as a *satirist* that Solondz presents his case—a category of artist that he understands in a classical sense: "Satire always has a moral underpinning," he insists, "an imperative to point out a flaw in a system or a character, and to expose its corruption, from the vantage point of what is right morally."[8] But as every true satirist since Jonathan Swift has painfully had to realize, "what is right morally" no longer has any stable point of reference in the spiritual substance of a people; rather, it can only be determined immanently, and negatively, through a process of ruthless and uncompromising subtraction from the official moral code of a mode of production that is inimical to morality itself. As Solondz has also had occasion to say, "The only true morality that exists in Hollywood is: if a movie is profitable it's a moral film, and if it isn't, it's not."[9] In order to deduce the outline of what a morally just principle might look like in the American cinema, therefore, one must perforate and travesty the "true morality of Hollywood" (profitability, the law of equivalence and exchange value) to such an extent that something like an inverted retinal impression of it might fluoresce behind the closed eyelids of refusal. Solondz's cinema begets that fluorescence; at war with itself, at war with the criteria of value that dominate its industry and nation, and at war with its own market, this cinema exudes the palpable idea of its own self-imposed exemption from the regime of value as such. "I can never presume that I'll ever make another movie," Solondz claims, "because I've lost too much money for too many people."[10] And each movie is a further twist in this same, self-defeating tale.

In what follows, we will track Solondz's canny cinematic homeopathy with the nation's overarching economic decline under the following rubrics: the built environment of his films, interested as they are in the aesthetically valueless architecture of junkspace; his stylistic posture of what I call "left classicism," which borrows key aesthetic principles from the dominant industry, only to drain them of their usual affirmative functions; his several ontological gestures of "eternal recurrence," offered with the twist of a general decline in standards; his determined interest in the dynamic opposition between playful sequences of fantasy and escape and unendurable long takes of truly intolerable material; and, finally, his thematic preoccupation with the excremental function of the gift, which he analyzes in an exhaustive fashion. It is to be hoped that with this multifaceted and synoptic approach to one of our great living satirists, we may come to a better understanding and a truer appreciation of a body of work that is too often dismissed with crude journalistic slogans and empty accusations of misanthropy.[11] On the contrary, as opposed to the countless artists in the cinema today who sully the idea of "humanism" with their trite and stereotypical depictions of nobility under adversity and sentimentality under the veneer of cynicism, Solondz will be seen to have been one of the rare few who stood by the conviction of every true satirist: that humanism in an inhuman world is a luxury none of us can afford.

Non-Place and How to Live There

It is notable that until the playful and ironic "Intermission" sequence from *Wiener-Dog* (2016), there is scarcely a recognizable landmark in all of Todd Solondz's work (though the Empire State Building makes a brief appearance in 1998's *Happiness*). And this is surely deliberate. In what pass for "establishing shots" in his films, the point is never to establish a knowable location, a "place," but only generic space; indeed, his establishing shots establish the disestablishment of all knowable coordinates.

This is the lived environment of his characters: not the glamorous, recognizable skylines of Manhattan or Chicago, or the sublime vistas of LA from the top of Mulholland Drive, but the anonymous strip malls, convenience stores, motels, looming megamalls and supermarkets, char-

Figure 1. *Happiness* (1998): establishing shot for Joy Jordan's call-center workplace

acterless apartment and office blocks, institutional hospital and school corridors, truck stops, chain restaurants, cheap diners, and bland suburban houses where his various dramatis personae dwell and labor, without any of what Henri Lefebvre called "representational space" to trigger durable, passionate attachments.[12] Such non-place is characterized by Rem Koolhaas as "Junkspace," for its essential disposability and the proliferating physical blight it imposes on a landscape.

> Junkspace is the body double of space, a Bermuda Triangle of concepts, an abandoned petri dish: it cancels distinctions, undermines resolve, confuses intention with realization. It replaces hierarchy with accumulation, composition with addition. More and more, more is more. . . . Patterns imply repetition or ultimately decipherable rules; Junkspace is beyond measure, beyond code. . . . Because it cannot be grasped, Junkspace cannot be remembered. . . . Its refusal to freeze ensures instant amnesia.[13]

Nothing here fascinates, nothing conducts psychic or affective energy, even the ubiquitous brand names and signage; nothing, it seems, could ever have happened in these history-repellent zones of the sprawl. Such space aborts any gesture toward human community, forcing instead a serial atomization of the public sphere. Here, in full view of everybody, one is subjected to routine "ordeals of solitude."[14] Strip-mall alienation hits a kind of peak in Solondz's *Happiness*, when Dr. Bill Maplewood rushes with a handful of boys' teen magazines to his vehicle in the mall parking lot, jumps into the rear seat, and frantically masturbates while a mother and children enter the adjacent car. Managing his pedophilic tendencies through a semipublic performance of mediated onanism, Dr. Maplewood exploits the crucial truth of non-place—its privatization of the public—to defer his victims' inevitable rapes. He is, as the Freudians say, a "criminal from a sense of guilt,"[15] driven by an a priori sense of shame to fulfill his inadmissible wishes in such a way as to "get caught"—but, of course, in non-place nobody gets caught. It is one of the features of this kind of built environment that, in it, nobody truly sees anyone else. Solondz tells the indicative story of trying to find a suitable place on the school premises during his location shoot for *Welcome to the Dollhouse* for the would-be rapist Brandon to threaten Dawn Wiener. But there was simply nowhere private enough—no dark corner or hidden passage—in the entire school (which had been designed along anti-bullying lines), so Solondz opted for the stark alternative: to shoot the scene in broad daylight outside one of the school exits, in full view of the practicing football team. Again, what is public in this space is always already fully privatized to the extent that nobody will see your worst excesses, even when enacted right under their noses.

The excess of signification in these non-places (the abundant signage, instructive ideograms, functionality of design, and so on) has the ironic effect of pressing them beyond the symbolic altogether, since they no longer anchor the participants in the spatial practices they sponsor in any singular world. "The property of symbolic universes is that they constitute a means of recognition, rather than knowledge, for those who have inherited them," observes anthropologist Marc Augé.[16] But in the post-symbolic spaces mapped by Solondz's films, the instability or absence of any coordinates for *collective* identification means that the burden is shifted more and more onto the *individual* who is obliged to map her own itinerary according to specific interests. To be sure, behind the back of this individual, the statistical patterns and logistical determinations of large-group movement under capitalism are carefully deliberated, but this collective is in all essentials invisible to itself, non-self-transparent, unbound by any ritual function or coherent concept to a social norm. With its masking, an ersatz freedom emerges. "Junkspace is a web without a spider; although it is an architecture of the masses, each trajectory is strictly unique. Its anarchy is one of the last tangible ways we experience freedom."[17]

When Remi (Keaton Nigel Cooke) and his mother, Dina (Julie Delpy), are driving to the vet to have the boy's new pet dog spayed in *Wiener-Dog*, we see through the windows of the family Subaru an endless, looping chain of strip malls, plazas, big-box centers, motels, chain restaurants, shopping malls, low-rise office blocks, and corporate distribution centers—the prototypical stretch of hastily built junkspace flung out along the busy arterials of so many suburban zones.

The architecture is devoid of any distinguishing features; its pale stucco and brick surfaces repel aesthetic attention, its abundant glass plainly reveals the commercial goods within or reflects the neighboring buildings, its signage is discrete, and the free parking just outside

Figure 2. *Wiener-Dog* (2016): the blur of non-place

traps commuters like gnats on flypaper. Its purpose here is to ramify the placeless commuter bubble that the car creates for this well-off family. Reflecting back nothing at them but their own indifference to social questions, the coagulating arterial architecture becomes a kind of vast, tasteless blur in their peripheral vision, blandly reassuring in its Teflon-like resistance to memory and passion.

Solondz, however, is less interested in scoring elitist points against this kind of junkspace than he is in asking how it is that we might, and indeed do, inhabit it. The bad press that strip malls in particular tend to attract in the ever intensifying push to gentrify more and more of the urbanosphere—"strip malls have been described as 'grim,' 'a war zone,' a 'wasteland,' a 'disaster,' or even simply dismissed as 'garbage'"[18]—functions in truth as an instrument of ruling-class pressure on the physical complexion of our cities. For all their aesthetic and existential pestilence, non-places like plazas and strip malls nevertheless allow smaller businesses to operate in populated areas, often with particular ethnic or religious appeals to otherwise neglected communities. The low-rent end of this space, in fact, enables lower-middle- and working-class suburbanites to make connections otherwise unavailable in the urban sprawl.

In *Wiener-Dog* the dog's first appearance in the urban wasteland of New Jersey (she starts her saga at a farmstead) is at a strip-mall veterinarian, whence all of its journeys are to follow. It is outside a strip-mall

Food Mart that the dog, now called Doody, waylays Brandon McCarthy (Kieran Culkin) and convinces him to take Dawn Wiener (Greta Gerwig) on the road. And it is at a nameless redbrick plaza that Dawn and Brandon will drop off the immigrant Mexican mariachi band that Doody had inspired them to pick up from a desolate roadside shoulder, having already spent the night with them in a cheap room at a Royale motel. The great error, the "wrong road taken," in the third part of the film, could thus be said to consist in the (now utterly nameless) dog's unwonted move to New York City, where there are no strip malls or chain motels to conduct the sympathies of the wayward, the homeless, and the lost, in the direction of redemption, and she is duly weaponized in the name of a despondent professional egotism.

Solondz's antielitist interest in modulating our knee-jerk dismissal of suburban non-place into something less disdainful—if never quite redeeming it—is ongoing and not confined to New Jersey. In a nocturnal dream sequence from *Life During Wartime* (2009), Joy Jordan (Shirley Henderson)—who is staying in an anonymous Florida hotel to escape the oppressive attentions of her mother—starts up and wanders somnambulistically out of the lobby, along a moon-drenched nature strip, across an empty parking lot, before the illuminated windows of a plaza, and into a generic, Hard Rock–styled restaurant. In her nightdress and quite alone, framed in a sequence of five fixed, elegant, medium-distance shots, and accompanied by a simple four-chord progression on the piano, she is almost beautiful. The space stretches out around her, unpopulated but romantic in its darkly heated expanses. This is non-place raised to the level of an existential absolute: traversed in isolation, abstracted from the grid of worldly concerns, handed over to the blankly generic. Solondz has said of Florida, "I call it the land of 'generica'—that sense of isolation and desolation within the wealth of the condominium world. Everywhere is nowhere is anywhere."[19] But in this sequence, the glass-concrete-and-stone of motel/plaza/chain-restaurant gives way under the pressure of reverie to a natural exteriority, conceived along the lines of a romantic painting. Joy has reclaimed junkspace in her dream and transformed it into a hallucinatory vision, one with significant affective appeal to the viewer.

Abe Wertheimer (Jordan Gelber) makes two visits to the Toys"R"Us big-box center during the course of *Dark Horse* (2011).[20] The first, filmed in bright morning sunshine, finds the parking lot sparsely used, giving

Figure 3. *Life During Wartime* (2009): Joy's moonscape, à la the Douanier Rousseau

the large rectangles of the store spatial prominence in the frame, its strong primary colors lit up by the sun like Abe's bright yellow Hummer. The second, placed much later in the film during the period of Abe's coma, and thus framed as a dark dream, takes place in pouring rain and a totally empty parking lot, resulting in muted tones and an exaggerated sense of foreboding as Abe trudges mechanically toward the entrance. The frame-ups of the two shots are almost identical, but the effects are startlingly different. The external non-place of the corporate big-box center demonstrates a capacity for variable affective investment: the difference between the well-defined outlines, colors, and shadows of the earlier shot and the muted, washed-out palette of the second suggests a late version of the "pathetic fallacy." Non-place is rarely filmed to extract from it this range of emotional tonalities; its cinematic function is generally to suggest purified commercial homogeneity, devoid of such variations of mood. There are not necessarily echoes of Monet's Rouen cathedral here, but in a rare act of empathy, Solondz has allowed a large chain store to signify more than the junkspace it so conspicuously is, to become complicate with a sentiment and a psyche not its own, to foster and conduct shifting affective intensities.

    That Abe should be singled out as especially sensitive to matters of space and the built environment is hardly surprising: he works for his father's family business in the property development line, although "works" is, to be sure, a matter of conjecture here. *Dark Horse* is Solondz's post-GFC film and is particularly interested in the economics and politics of place after the 2008 meltdown in the US property market. Both Abe and his betrothed, Miranda (Selma Blair, formerly "Vi," from *Storytelling* [2001]), live at home in their parents' suburban houses, a three-hour drive apart. Neither has the economic clout to leave the family nest or, with the bursting of the housing bubble, the incentive to do so. As Abe puts it to his (here, fantasized, Ferrari-driving) office mate Marie (Donna Murphy), "It costs *a lot* of money to move out! I'm not rich!" The luxurious house where he points this out is Abe's fantasized projection of the haute-bourgeois domicile in late-capitalist America: lots of glass, white-brick walls in the entrance corridor, lap pool, mood lighting over the foyer sculpture, and a Franz Kline painting hung over the remote-control fireplace. "All this time I'd imagined you living in some . . . depressing place," says Abe, "with, I dunno, stuffed animals and pictures of cats!" (It transpires, in the film's moving epilogue, that this is precisely where she does live, in a run-down suburban two-story wood-frame house backing on to a raised highway—though Abe has neglected to predict the inevitable posters for Broadway musicals.) But now dream-Marie informs him: "I got it after I sold the estate; your father helped me out." Abe's spatial imaginary is structured by the Oedipal struggles he has with his "asshole" property-investor father, Jackie (Christopher Walken), and overdetermined by a financial dependency he can never surmount.[21]

The family firm is working on a major property deal, the Eastlake development, which their lawyer, Phil (in a scene to which Abe shows up late), outlines as an opportunity for smart profiteering: funding the various sellers until they can get approval, submitting a wetlands delineation, doing the Phase One environmental report, and then swooping on a number of adjacent properties once things come together, "so we can get contingent uses." The scene, set in a small sky-blue conference room with whiteboard and potted ferns, is a fly-on-the-wall exposé of the tedious machinations and contrivances, and the colorless jargon, that make property development and management such a driver of what remains of the US economy. The final shot in the film—a single, decorous reverse dolly focusing on Marie in the firm's reception area,

14 | **Todd Solondz**

snapping out of her reverie about the dead Abe—retreats just enough to take in the adjacent office, where Jackie (framed in the doorway) and cousin Justin (Zachary Booth, framed in the window) are still going over the details of the Eastlake deal. The genius of the brief sequence lies in the discordance felt between our immersion in the affective truth of Marie's melancholy (we begin in a close-up of her face) and the murmuring background static of a barely audible workplace conversation, which rattles relentlessly on and spits in the face of our concern for poor Marie, before cutting to black and the credit roll:

JACKIE: . . . to finish the spreadsheets.
JUSTIN: Uh, sure thing, Uncle Jackie.
JACKIE: Show me what you got.
JUSTIN: Here you go. It's a list of all the units of property.
JACKIE: Has that nail salon paid up?
JUSTIN: Uh, no, we're still waiting for a final payment.
JACKIE: Call Phil again, tell him to follow up. Draw up eviction papers. What about the bagel place? The attorneys get back to you?
JUSTIN: Yes, they requested that we move the court date to the end of next month.
JACKIE: And the dry cleaners . . . they're gonna pass the environmental, or they still working on the clean-up?
JUSTIN: The work is done. They're just waiting for the inspectors.

Figure 4. *Dark Horse* (2011): the haunting final shot, with Marie, Jackie, and Justin

JACKIE: Ask Phil what he can do to speed things up. I don't want Eastlake to fall apart.

JUSTIN: Uh-huh. Of course, of course, Uncle Jackie.

Cousin Justin, the eternal "yes-man," has replaced Abe, the naysaying Oedipal thorn in the side of the firm, and the wheels are greased to rotate eternally, evicting late-paying clients, artificially accelerating reports, and generally defrauding the public of its entitlement to habitable civic space. Of course, we know exactly (or think we know) what kind of development Eastlake is to be; even Miranda's parents sniff it out spontaneously:

DAD: So what do you do for a living?

ABE: Got a company. Work in real estate. Property management, commercial developments . . .

MOM: You mean, like all those strip malls?

ABE: Mm-hm.

MOM: Where there used to be parks and mom-and-pop stores.

Yet things are never quite so clear. As we have seen, strip malls themselves, and their cognate structures of arterial spatial congestion, do not simply cancel civic space as such but here and there revive it in a logic of contingency that the films have a stake in rehearsing. There is, in fact, the hint of a suggestion that it is precisely a strip mall—bagel shop, dry cleaners, and so forth—that the family firm is engaged in buying out in order to "upgrade" into a more aesthetically and commercially viable urban form. Indeed, it is this very process of incessant upgrade and renovation that *Dark Horse* is especially concerned to contest.

When taking Miranda on her first tour of the Wertheimer home, Abe is moved to comment that the ink lines on a door frame marking his and his brother Richard's successive heights during their childhood were wallpapered over by his father's first redecoration, as if, in a logic stemming from the "creative destruction" of the built environment where Jackie makes his living, even home renovation translates into family amnesia and the repression of all affective traces. But that is not to say that the repressed cannot return. For in Abe's last act of consciousness, he returns as a ghostly revenant to the home he has always lived in (from the hospital bed where he lies dying) to that same door frame, where the staggered height marks are visible once more, and a loose flap of wallpaper is peeled back to reveal the film's emotional depth charge in extreme close-up: an archaeological memento of Jackie's abandoned sentimental feelings for his eldest son—the legend "Abe—6/93—Dad's 'Dark Horse,'" the term he reserves for the worthiest competitors, provided they turn out winners. There is, then, a countervailing force at work here, chewing occasional wormholes through a ubiquitous junkspace into the vanishing spiritual substance interred beneath its constantly renovated surfaces.

That force is allied closely with death. Approaching the far end of adulthood, or emerging beyond it into old age, the body engages nonplace with a relative indifference to the protocols of pseudo-conviviality and collective amnesia programmed by the designers. In one of the strongest scenes he ever mounted, for *Life During Wartime*, Solondz abandons a skulking Dr. Bill Maplewood (Ciarán Hinds) to the predations of cinema's most nihilistic barfly, played with chill elegance by Charlotte Rampling. The scene plays out at a small hotel bar table, and a room upstairs without a view ("Who the fuck needs one anyway?"); lit in low-key side lighting and suffused with the warm gold and green colors that define this film's chromatic field, it details a rapid seduction and tryst. What these two monsters do to the space they occupy beggars description; the death drive that operates through them, transmuted into malice and unassuageable grief, bores holes into the non-place of the hotel, perforating its slick sheen with thrusts of ferocious negation. It is one of several episodes in Solondz's work where the anonymous corporate décor—designed to flatten all the human feeling that passes through it in a day into cosmetic advertisements for itself—is host to a surge in emotional violence so savage that it short-circuits the scenery.

Most infamous of these is the opening sequence of *Happiness*—a scene that he reprised, with variations, for the opening of *Life During Wartime* (as we shall see). Here, in the "three-and-a-half star" restaurant where Andy Kornbluth (Jon Lovitz) has taken Joy Jordan (Jane Adams) on their second date, the décor is so oppressively schmaltzy and "cheerful" (pink tablecloths and napkins, festoons of arranged lilies, a banquette upholstery that seems ripped from the floor of a 1970s Cincinnati hotel lobby) that it promises to neutralize all meaningful exchange in advance. But in a stunning in medias res opening close-up of Joy's anxious, quivering face, and the moist-eyed reverse-shot close-up of Andy that follows it, we are given to understand that the bomb has already detonated, setting off an emotional chain reaction that this kitschy interior design was never intended to absorb. Tears, snot, and phlegm rise rapidly to the surface of the supremely awkward breakup conversation—excremental body stuff implicitly forbidden by the anodyne civility of this space—followed by a volley of verbal ferocity and abuse that we will analyze later in another context. The point to note here is how this atrocious encounter, tending toward death (Andy will have killed himself within days), grates against the interior surfaces of the non-place where it happens, wearing away its coded imperturbability, its "colossal security blanket,"[22] to expose the raw nerve ends of violent interpersonal affectivity beneath. It is telling that in a later scene Joy's sisters, Trish (Cynthia Stevenson) and Helen (Lara Flynn Boyle), visit the same restaurant, to Helen's griping: "I don't know why I suggested this place; Joy recommended it." They are seated at a table positioned just in front of the banquette where Joy and Andy have had their last supper only two days before, the site of emotional crimes so dire that they literally entail a body count. (*Life During Wartime* adds Allen, Joy's future husband, to the mortal victims of this same banquette.) It takes a moment to realize that this recommendation must have followed the scene we have already witnessed, that Joy has either repressed her trauma or secretly wished its spatial reverberations upon her siblings. Lit up by sunshine and full of the professional lunch crowd, the décor has reclaimed its placeless serenity from the emotional shambles to which Andy had reduced it—enough, anyway, to stage the casual back-and-forth egotism and rivalry of the two elder Jordan sisters.

Solondz works harder than most directors, then, to invest suburban non-place with the affective range usually associated with the architecture of larger urban concentrations: complex valences of mood most often written off in the sprawling, build-by-numbers hinterland of our big cities. But at the very lowest, dilapidated end of this junk–architecture continuum, he discovers the more existential menace of a true class difference, as experienced by his suburbanites on the road. En route to his brother's house in Ohio to bring word of their father's death, Brandon McCarthy in *Wiener-Dog* stops off with Dawn at his uncle's ruinous domicile in some perfectly anonymous backwater of the American

Figure 5. *Wiener-Dog* (2016): where the poor live

dream. Raised by concrete from the weed-infested earth, embedded in the dusky woods amid the sounds of cicadas, crickets, and a barking dog, a long, low-slung wall of prefabricated wood-veneer vertical slats, stained with age and wear, stares blankly at us with as much grim threat as melancholy. This is the peripheral dwelling place of America's working poor, which we sense as an outer limit to Solondz's suburban universe.

There is to be no encounter, no catharsis here, but, of course, Brandon (whose run-down house on the outskirts of town in *Welcome to the Dollhouse* is already a step in this direction) accepts it as the shape of his destiny while Dawn looks on in anxious uncertainty from the car's shotgun window.

Solondz's only true "road movie," *Palindromes*, repeatedly flirts with this blasted kind of space: first in the "Budget 19" truck-stop motel-diner—shot unusually from a high angle—where "Henrietta" Aviva (Rachel Corr) and her trucker escort "Joe" (Stephen Adly Guirgi) first couple; second, at the dilapidated farmstead where Peter Paul (Alexander Brickel) takes "Mama Sunshine" Aviva (Sharon Wilkins) to show her the aborted fetuses; and third, the rusting trailer home on cinder blocks outside Mama Sunshine's where "Bob" Aviva (Shayna Levine) meets Bob/Earl/Joe again. This is the transient environment of economic contraction and systemic foreclosure, the bad conscience of a growth-addled suburban sprawl, where American optimism gives up the ghost and the promise of individual fulfillment is broken. It is working-class space, but there is nobody home, nobody to do the work, except itinerant exiles in a downward-tending class mobility defined by drift and entropy. It is the kind of space, we gather, into which Bill Maplewood himself is inevitably moving by the close of *Life During Wartime*, the former affluent professional last glimpsed in a furtive apparition skulking along a suburban sidewalk, and with nowhere (as an ex-con with no income) to go but this crumbling wasteland of the American underemployed.

However, the surest test of suburban non-place is not the exploration of its outer limits but the way it is inhabited, not by its native Jewish and WASP denizens, but by the Other as such; and here the supreme test case is that of the Salvadoran domestic servant Consuelo (Lupe Ontiveros), in Solondz's harshest work, *Storytelling*. Our first introduction to the locus classicus of this film's second part—"Non-Fiction"—the interior of the Livingston residence in Livingston, New Jersey (itself the locus classicus of the Solondz universe), is a medium shot of the family at the dinner table awaiting the arrival of their eldest son, Scooby (whom we understand, through the muffled soundtrack of camp 1980s-era Elton John, to be upstairs in his room), into which prototypical sitcom tableau shambles the melancholy figure of Consuelo, delivering a covered tray of warm rolls. Thus does the large, architect-designed, suburban three-

Figure 6. *Palindromes* (2004): a shuttered truck-stop diner

story Livingston home disclose the lugubrious "servant's hand" toiling at its hearth.[23] Consuelo makes no pretense at being a happy worker. Her shuffling gait, labored breath, downcast expression, unkempt appearance, and surly silence delineate the shape of her character as the dejected bad conscience of the sunny TV family. But Solondz is not content for this presence to wander dolefully in the film's margins; rather, he wants to draw her into the main action of the film through one of his signature devices: the repeated, protracted conversation between child and adult on topics that never get an airing on the laugh-track comedies these situations parodically resemble.

Here the scenes of dialogue occur between Consuelo and the family's youngest son, the absurdly precocious and thoroughly disagreeable Mikey (Jonathan Osser). The first of these takes place the next day, after a panning shot at waist height discovers Consuelo on hands and knees scrubbing at something on the kitchen floor, thus justifying the Ozu-level elevation. The "something" turns out, on a cut to an over-the-shoulder shot from Mikey's point of view as he comes to speak with her, to be dog shit, at which she huffs and puffs with audible displeasure. The shot/reverse-shot editing that structures the subsequent dialogue alternates between alarming low-angle shots of Mikey's looming class authority and that same over-the-shoulder high-angle shot of Consuelo on all fours sponging at the excrement, looking up only once from her task to deliver the final line in this exchange with a savage glare:

MIKEY: Consuelo?
CONSUELO: Yes, Mikey?
MIKEY: Do you have any brothers or sisters?
CONSUELO: Yes. [. . .] Four brothers and five sisters.
MIKEY: Wow. Why did your parents have so many children? I mean, if they were poor, wouldn't it be better to have just one or two?
CONSUELO: It was God's will.
MIKEY: But do you really believe in God? Heaven, hell, and angels and all that kind of stuff.
CONSUELO: [Pause, staring at him.] No.

The spatial politics of the scene are self-evident: Consuelo's place is on the floor with the filth while Mikey observes dispassionately from the elevation of his privilege, even as a ten-year-old child. But it is the way the dialogue exacerbates these underlying class tectonics with Mikey's unthinking malice, and Consuelo's laconic obedience to the rules of the game, that lifts these scenes out of mere satire and into a different level of intensity than the rest of the film. What matters most here is that the visiting documentarian, Toby Oxman (Paul Giamatti), precisely fails to see Consuelo in this way because of his preconceived conviction that the film to be made in the Livingston home is all about *Scooby*—about the college admissions system and the place of white youth in suburbia. "Either Scooby is the focus, or forget it," Mr. Livingston (John Goodman) barks at Oxman on their first interview as Consuelo shuffles in with a trayful of Twinkies and tea, and the point is made yet again. There is one kind of film (Oxman's) that will merely see Consuelo as a background figure, an adjunct to the space that contains and employs her, and another (Solondz's) that will raise her into a speaking part and indeed allow her the film's most extraordinary agency within this space, as we shall see.

This is not entirely true, of course, and the first time we find Oxman and his cameraman installed in the Livingston home, they are filming a shot of Mrs. Livingston (Julie Hagerty) raising funds for the new wing at Beth Israel hospital on the kitchen telephone, while in the background (and out of focus) Consuelo dusts the living-room curtains. To the extent that Solondz's camera mimics the viewfinder in Mike's handheld VHS camera, what we thus perceive is class comedy at its broadest: a middle-class woman raising charity money from (and for) other middle-class women while the working-class woman toils thanklessly at the rear of frame. But then suddenly, in the depth of our shot, we see Oxman and Mikey setting up a new shot at Consuelo's side, and we cut to it—a jerky, handheld videotape close-up of Consuelo's perspiring face, breathing hard, hand wiping at her brow. So the documentarian at least perceives some of the sociological depths of this space and is prepared to clear a certain area of his work for the figure of the laborer in its midst. But that she should remain speechless, a pitiable silent reproach to middle-class existence, marks the limit of Oxman's compassion and his social vision. He sees no drama here, no narrative depth, only a mute irony to be played for a combination of laughs and sighs, because he does not perceive suburban space as a site of true class struggle. (He also completely misses Scooby's budding homosexuality.) The film framing his film, on the other hand, has a far more serious message about the persistence of class struggle in the very place—suburbia—where America has dissimulated its obsolescence.

The second installment of Mikey and Consuelo's three-part conversation happens after Brady's football accident and hospitalization, and it concerns the question of work—her work in particular. Throughout the short scene, Consuelo is constantly moving, cleaning at the sink, wiping the stovetop, putting leftovers in the fridge off-screen, as her unexpressive face allows the thoughtless cruelty of Mikey's lines to run like water off a duck's back.

> MIKEY: What did you do in high school?
> CONSUELO: I did not go to high school.
> MIKEY: Weren't there high schools in El Salvador?
> CONSUELO: We had to work. My family was poor.
> MIKEY: It must have been hard being poor.
> CONSUELO: I'm still poor.
> MIKEY: But, Consuelo, even though you're poor, don't you have any hobbies or interests or anything?
> CONSUELO: No, Mikey.
> MIKEY: But like, what do you like to do when you're not working?
> CONSUELO: I am always working.
> MIKEY: But when you're not. Like now. What do you like to do?
> CONSUELO: This is work.
> MIKEY: But it's not like *real* work. This is just babysitting.
> CONSUELO: [*Looks up silently at him.*]
> MIKEY: You know, your job's really not so bad, if you think about it. You should smile more often.

While the dialogue opens up a seam of deep empathy against the grain of Mikey's condescending interrogation—in the glimpse it affords of Consuelo's youthful poverty and escalating alienation—the staging and blocking of the scene makes an even more powerful point: that there is no surface, no nook or cranny, of the Livingston home that is not a site of the extraction of surplus value from the exploited labor of this woman immigrant. "I am always working" works so poignantly as a line, to the extent that it is a summative description of exactly what we constantly see her doing on the screen, and because it extends to the enunciation of the line itself, for it transpires that the most challenging part of her 24/7 labor regimen consists in this interminable "babysitting" of a child who routinely humiliates her through the very ardency of his interlocutory concern for her.

Affluent suburban space is a punishing shop floor for the domestic workers who keep it so spotless, gleaming, and sanitized. It has been abundantly documented that very few legal protections are available to such workers, without whom suburbia would simply collapse. These mostly immigrant women are routinely paid at well under the minimum wage, which itself does not provide an adequate living; they receive no health care provision or retirement benefits; and they are prevented from living with their families by the expectation that they will dwell in their employer's house. Ten years after the release of *Storytelling* the figures were as stark as ever (see Table 1).

The live-in Latina with cleaning and nanny duties is thus placed at the very bottom of the ladder of domestic labor in the United States. That Consuelo is expected to work to a 24/7 time clock on an unlivable wage amid the smells of her oppressors is brought savagely home at the final encounter between these two, when, during a late-night visit to the refrigerator, Mikey spills a jug of grape juice on the spotless kitchen floor. His first instinct is to freeze, face off-screen, and shout out "Consuelo!" When there is no answer, Mikey goes in search of his redoubtable drudge and tracks her down to her lair, a tiny basement cell behind the sports trophy collections and rumpus room, where she is weeping quietly. It turns out that her grandson Jésus has been on death row for rape and murder and has just today been executed with poison gas. But her grief extorts no sympathy from her tormentor. After a long, appalling exchange

Table 1. Median hourly wage for occupations by race/ethnicity and employment arrangement

		Nannies	Caregivers	Housecleaners	All Occupations
Race/Ethnicity:	White	$12.55	$12.00	$12.50	$12.13
	Latina/o	$8.57	$10.00	$10.00	$10.00
	Black	$12.71	$10.00	$10.89	$10.99
	Asian/Other	$11.11	$8.33	$10.00	$10.00
Live-in/out:	Live-in	$6.76	$7.69	$5.12	$6.15
	Live-out	$11.55	$10.00	$10.71	$10.82
All Workers		$11.00	$10.00	$10.00	$10.00

Source: Analysis of 2011–2012 National Domestic Workers Survey

during which he wonders whether the execution might be for the best and approves of the death penalty, Mikey concludes their colloquy with the inevitable request: "Consuelo, I spilled some grape juice upstairs. Do you think you could clean up the floor now?"

So it is that in the film's totally unexpected denouement, it is Consuelo herself (now sacked thanks to Mikey's intervention), and not Scooby, who ties up the dangling narrative threads. During Scooby's unhappy trip to the big city to catch a test screening of "American Scooby" (in which, crucially, we do not see her once), Consuelo returns to chez Livingston while all four indoors are asleep—Brady in his vegetative abyss, and Mikey curled up between his mother and father in the conjugal bed, "monster-proofed." Only not really, not at all, because the monster he has made is now a vengeful revenant armed with a front-door key, the household towels, and a working knowledge of the gas supply. In one of the critical long takes of his career, Solondz holds for thirty-four interminable seconds on an external shot of the suburban home as Consuelo slips away into the night and the gas hisses its sinister secrets to the dreaming Livingstons, who will never wake again. Scooby's return by bus the next morning finally reveals that this massive suburban house, which has become a multiple-murder site, is located in a gated community—"Misty Grove"—where the shell-shocked neighbors gather to watch the paramedics hauling out the body bags. It is perfectly apposite that Scooby should this morning wear a maroon "CCCP" T-shirt with the hammer and sickle on prominent display, since this traumatizing event (which hurts him less than Oxman's test screening has) is one of those "now hidden, now open" incidents of what Karl Marx called the uninterrupted fight between the classes "that each time ended, either in a revolutionary reconstitution of society at large or in the common ruin of the contending classes."[24] Class struggle has come to the suburbs not as a conflagration of tenement buildings, ripped-up cobblestones, and the urgent massing of urban bodies but as a toxic whisper in the night and the quiet industry of the emergency services by morning.

Left Classicism

Critics of Solondz who like to think of him as so preoccupied by the exigencies of story and character creation that the other, more obviously stylistic and visual aspects of filmmaking assume little or no importance in his work are very much mistaken, though not without good reason. The great cinematographer Ed Lachman, who worked with Solondz on two features, *Life During Wartime* and *Wiener-Dog*, approached their first association with this same hesitancy:

> I knew Todd's work before I had the opportunity to work with him. . . . Up until what we did in *Life During Wartime*, I found his imagery very minimalistic. In a strange way I almost had a trepidation about working with him, because I felt, because of his storytelling and because of his writing, that he was more interested in the arc of his stories and the characters than he was in the images. But I realized it's just that he didn't want his images to overshadow what his basic interest is in the characters. I think he always wanted me, visually, to *take out* things about the images, to bring the people forward. He allowed me to find, with him, a visual equivalent of what his stories were about.[25]

The maestro of Todd Haynes's *I'm Not There* (2007) and *Carol* (2015), maker of Sophia Coppola's reputation on *The Virgin Suicides* (1999), two-time collaborator with Robert Altman, and Steven Soderbergh's camera eye on *Erin Brockovich* (2000) thus tended to associate Solondz in advance with a nonvisual style offering little enough incentive to his talents as one of America's most adventurous directors of photography. But here the terms of engagement are already adumbrated: minimalism, subtraction, and equivalence. What Solondz appears primarily concerned with at the level of cinematography is that it become a nonostentatious vessel for narrative materials that are themselves already "charged" with an excess of connotation and consequence. As he insists in the interview given for this volume, "It's about pulling back as much as possible, to trust the text itself, to trust the context and the actors. I don't want to call attention to what's already there in a self-conscious way." The goal is what he calls a "restrained simplicity," such that the camera never draws attention to itself in a way that might distract us from the material it is framing. The cinematography adheres to an ethic of *subtraction*, achieving a certain visual *minimalism* in whose imagery the "style" is ideally *equivalent* to the "content." Nothing is so simple, of course, and there are all kinds of exceptions to this rule, as we shall see, but that it is a rule, resulting in a consistency of presentation across the entire oeuvre with few comparable cases in cinema history, is scarcely deniable.[26]

It is worth dwelling on what is most exceptional about this formidable stylistic restraint in the context of independent American cinema. For in the United States, the hegemonic instance of the Hollywood studio system is so preponderant that independent filmmakers have typically sought to forge their aesthetic signatures on the basis of its studious negation: longer takes, Dutch angles, handheld cameras, swooping dollies, illogical cuts, and so on—in other words, the elaboration of an exorbitant and self-conscious visual style militating against the "classical continuity system" and the puritanical discourse of Hollywood's narrative juggernaut. Think of Spike Lee's bold compositions and off-center close-ups, John Cassavetes's handheld documentary-style cameras and bad sound mixes, Andy Warhol's infinite takes and amateur lenses, Maya Deren's multiple exposures and jump cuts, or John Waters's imperfect lighting and muddy colorations. Some of this is evident in Solondz's disowned and disastrous first feature film, *Fear, Anxiety, and Depression* (1989), about which a few things now need to be said, though Solondz has duly cautioned everybody to avoid it at all costs.

For it is clear that with this first funded feature-length project, Solondz was aiming for a "zany," next-generation reboot of the *Annie Hall*–era (1977) Woody Allen–style Manhattan comedy: full of roving street-level dollies, wild high-angle shots, point-of-view shots, broadly exaggerated performances, rent-controlled bohemian locales, addresses to camera, and a stuttering, neurotic central performance by Solondz himself. The film thus bristles with all the "indy" style signatures that an aspiring auteur of the late 1980s might wish to leave as calling cards to the industry, backed by the reassurance of an underlying familiarity. Allen—the Jewish American cinema's premier postwar comic talent—had evidently hijacked Solondz's more abiding affiliation with the art cinemas of George Kuchar, Kenneth Anger, and Andy Warhol so that all the more perverse and daring elements of his scenario were projected through a recognizable modal and affective scrim, which tended to override the film's compact with its audience. At any rate, it is not a film characterized by any restraint whatsoever, and this perhaps serves as a key to the rest of Solondz's oeuvre, which with one significant exception is held together by the exceptional consistency of "restrained simplicity"—of camera movement, camera placement, movement inside the frame, and so forth—as if in ongoing repudiation and disavowal of his first outing as a director.

That exception, *Welcome to the Dollhouse*, must therefore be construed as the "work of transition," so conspicuous is it as a via media between the stylistic excess and self-consciousness of *Fear, Anxiety, and Depression* and the canonical "straightness" of *Happiness*. In *Dollhouse*, indeed, we note a definite and forced mutation of the visual language, without yet a full evolutionary leap into what I am going to be analyzing as Solondz's mature *classicism* of formal means.

Consider the opening three minutes of *Welcome to the Dollhouse*. After a title sequence that boldly announces Solondz's oddly classical intentions for a high school movie (title cards in flowing calligraphic script, a fully framed family portrait photograph on which the camera steadily closes in to a close-up of Dawn Wiener's [Heather Matarazzo's] grinning face, all to the pianoforte strains of Chopin's Waltz in A-flat Major, "L'Adieu"), we cut to a right-panning shot of a packed school cafeteria at lunchtime, which ends its arc on the forlorn, solitary figure of Dawn in medium shot, lunch tray in hand, looking for somewhere to sit and eat. The shot next switches track into a semi-orbital dolly around Dawn, from her left side to her front, and then commences a slow reverse track as she walks despondently toward us, in search of a seat. A cut interpolates a reverse point-of-view (POV) shot that shows a boy diving into an available seat and smirking up the camera. We then cut back to the backward traveling shot of Dawn, still looking, moving farther into the cafeteria hall. Cut to another interpolated traveling POV shot framing a girl jumping into another available seat. And again we cut back to the reverse dolly shot of Dawn, who now pauses, clearly seeing something, heaves a deep sigh, and moves forward to the left of screen, where a camera pan reveals an almost empty table. "Can I sit here?," she asks, and we cut one last time to a POV shot of the only girl at the table, the bully Lolita, who stares malevolently up at us, waits a beat, and replies, "If you feel like it." What is striking about this sequence is its movement: constant, fluid, and choreographed with a rhythmic precision to bring out the horror of occupying the bottom place in the school hierarchy. Yet this is something Solondz will refrain from repeating in his later films; there is too much self-consciousness, too much regard for the

28 | **Todd Solondz**

camera as a semi-autonomous agent in the busy space, too much "wit" in the shot/reverse-shot structure of the cutting. It is an effective and memorable opening sequence, but it bears the imprints of an authorial wish to impress, a hovering flair over and above the material itself.

Later in the film, too, Solondz makes shot selections that comment dryly on the material rather than simply depicting it. In the scene where Dawn detains Steve Rodgers (Eric Mabius) with her piano-playing skills, we see, first, a slowly approaching dolly of Dawn's back seated at the stool, hammering out a wretchedly incompetent assay on that same Chopin waltz, on a piano that hasn't been tuned in years. Next we get a close-up of Dawn's face as she plays, slowly dollying left, showing her deep concentration. And finally a reverse-angle cut to a medium shot of her back again as she concludes the piece but also framing Steve's munching profile in the foreground, allowing their dialogue to be tagged to shifts in the focal range as each character is pulled into focus by the fact of speaking lines. Later still there is the montage of alternating lateral right-left/left-right tracks in the school as the countdown to rape at 3:00 PM is on, each establishing a dynamic interplay between Dawn and Brandon (Brendan Sexton III), rounded up by a whip pan from the clock face set at 2:59 to Dawn's anxious backward glance. And as one last illustration, the colorful anniversary sequence features a camera that roams of its own accord from the airbrushed double-portrait cake, to the couple it depicts, to the wider crowd, and finally floats up above the fray to single out Dawn framed in her upstairs window, looking down miserably at the proceedings. These shots, once again, signal more than mere attention to the material and attest to that quasi-autonomous visual pleasure taken in movement and play with depth of field, of the sort that Solondz will later deem inadmissible. They are subtle enough, to be sure, in the annals of independent American cinema, but they portend a certain will to style that militates against an ethic of subtraction and equivalence.

Yet that ethic, too, is steadily at work in this film, in any number of ways. Specifically, it settles on the scenes structured around dialogue, and we can therefore make an a posteriori distinction between the dialogue-based scenes and the sequences discussed above—which are more illustrative, summative, or iterative in narrative function. We can then correlate that distinction with the modulation between a more flamboyant style for the transitional or descriptive passages and the neutral, subtractive style that defines the scenes themselves. There is no better instance of the mature Solondz scenographic style at its inception than in the cinematography and editing of the film's standout scene, between Dawn and Brandon outside an abandoned building, where the threatened rape is due to take place. These are the shots that comprise its three-minute duration:

1. (42:27–43:10 = 43 seconds) EXT: very long-distance shot of DAWN and BRANDON walking left along an abandoned road, along a chain-link fence marked KEEP OUT, erected around some abandoned buildings, which pans left with them until they reach an opening in the fence, then stops and allows them to enter. The lyrical melody of Edvard Grieg's "Solveig's Song" plays over the shot. Once they are within the location, the music fades out and their dialogue commences; we see only their tiny children's bodies at a great distance, while the soundtrack leans right in:

   DAWN: Do you want me to lie down?
   BRANDON: OK.

2. (43:10–43:35 = 25 seconds) EXT: medium shot of DAWN and BRAN-DON sitting down in the abandoned yard, he on a rock, she on an old mattress where she reclines. He takes out a pack of cigarettes and lights up. A ruined old chest of drawers and lawnmower are visible on the grass.

   BRANDON: Want a smoke first?
   DAWN: No, thanks.
   BRANDON: Afraid?
   DAWN: No, I just don't feel like it. (*Sitting up, pulling the camera slightly right.*) But I think marijuana should be legalized.

3. (43:35–43:47 = 12 seconds) EXT: reverse-angle medium shot of BRAN-DON seated to left of screen reacting to DAWN, right, slightly out of focus in the foreground.

   BRANDON: Why do you always have to be such a cunt?

   He stands up and walks left, the camera tilting up and panning to follow him to the fence, where he stops, his arms leaning on the fence.

4. (43:47–43:52 = 5 seconds) EXT: reverse-angle shot of DAWN, still

seated, framed to right, with the vacant spot to the left where BRAN-DON used to be, unbalancing the composition.

DAWN: I'm sorry. Brandon, I don't mean to be a cunt.

5. (43:52–43:56 = 4 seconds) EXT: reverse-angle shot of BRANDON, still leaning on the fence, back to camera. A shift in mood.

BRANDON: You know I've got a brother?

6. (43:56–43:59 = 3 seconds) EXT: same as 4, above.

DAWN: No, I never knew that. What grade's he in?

7. (43:59–44:04 = 5 seconds) EXT: same as 5, above.

BRANDON: He's not in any grade. He's retarded.

8. (44:03–44:10 = 7 seconds) EXT: Close-up of DAWN reacting to Brandon's news, still positioned to the right of frame.

DAWN: Oh.

She makes to get up, and the camera starts following her.

9. (44:10–45:21 = 71 seconds) EXT: close-up of BRANDON's face, sharply focused, positioned left of frame and looking off left, his left hand gripping the top of the fence. In the background, out of focus, DAWN gets up and walks to middle distance over his left shoulder. The camera subtly shifts right to accommodate her, but she remains out of focus.

DAWN: I'm sorry.
BRANDON: There's nothing to be sorry about. He's a tough kid. He could beat you up if he wanted.

DAWN moves slightly closer, to right of frame, still out of focus. He looks back at her. She moves up into a full two-shot, both children framed behind the top of the chain-link fence, the camera becoming properly frontal.

DAWN: I'm sorry. I mean. Yeah.

BRANDON suddenly leans to his left to kiss her. The camera swoops in, right, to capture this kiss as the fence drops out of frame. He pulls back, they breathe. He moves in and kisses her again, fuller this time. The camera pulls back to its previous position, the fence showing again.

DAWN: Brandon. Are you still going to rape me?
BRANDON: What time is it?

DAWN: I dunno. But I guess I don't have to be home yet.
BRANDON: Nah, there's not enough time.
DAWN: Thanks, Brandon.

He moves into her again, this time quasi-threateningly, and the camera repeats its lunge in so that the top of the fence falls out of frame again.

BRANDON: Yeah, but just remember, this didn't happen. I mean no one, fucking no one.
DAWN: I swear I won't tell anybody, not a soul.
BRANDON: 'Cause if you do, I really will rape you next time.

His face is now pressed directly into hers, in a gesture both tender and intimidating.
Cut.

There is a great deal to be said about this, one of the outstanding scenes of American cinema in the 1990s. The rhythm of the shot lengths is exceptionally precise: for the first four shots, each is roughly half the length of the previous one (40:20:10:5); the next four shots last an average of 4.5 seconds as the dialogue between separated parties accelerates, while the final shot, a mesmerizing 71 seconds long, establishes the proper coming together of these unlikely lovers.

This expert rhythm of contraction and explosion, of division and reunification, is unlike anything else in the film. But we also need to acknowledge the equally adroit handling of shot distance in this scene, moving from an extreme long distance, through medium distance, into an exquisite byplay of close-ups and a two-shot. Focus becomes an important element toward the end of the sequence. And the compositions are ravishingly clear in their decisions about weighting, distribution, and relative values within the frame. Throughout, too, the movement of the camera is judiciously poised and calibrated to key points of the conversation, while movements within the frame subtly ramify the escalating emotional temperature of the scene.

Here we reach the gist of the matter. For this is one of two scenes in the film that actually touches a powerful emotional core: the star-crossed love growing between the former class enemies—working-class Brandon and middle-class Dawn—against the violent background of

Todd Solondz

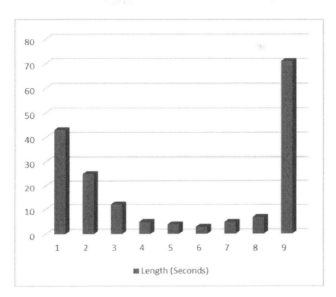

Chart 4. Shot lengths of "Dawn and Brandon's first kiss" scene in *Welcome to the Dollhouse* (1995)

bullying and the discourse of rape. In all other sequences—the various offenses at school, the rivalry with Missy at home, the crush on Steve, the dismantlement of the clubhouse, the rescue mission to the city, and the trip to Disneyland—the material may be excruciating and painful, yet the tone is distinctly ironic, and the mood vacillates between hilarity and shock. But in the two critical scenes between Dawn and Brandon outside school grounds, it is imperative that this prevailing tone and this comic range of moods be adjusted to suit a far more resonant affective repertoire: tenderness, vulnerability, honesty, and shared pain. And to orchestrate that shift, as he does masterfully in this scene, Solondz avails himself of a distinctive aesthetic approach to framing, moving, and cutting. No longer indulging playful, self-conscious, quasi-autonomous cinematographic gestures or "punch line" cutting, here he exercises the kind of stylistic restraint that will henceforth define his cinema. There is not a pan or tilt out of place, each keyed to the growing intimacy between the protagonists, and the dialogue plays against cuts that amplify rather than defray its unspoken resonance.

Consider the exchange over the word "cunt." In another scene it would have played only for laughs, but here, due to the circumambient mood created by the varying shot lengths and shot distances, its force is powerfully affirmative. In the interview for this book, Solondz himself remarks:

> To me, what's poetry is when the bully says to Dawn Wiener, "Why do you have to be such a cunt?" And she says "I don't mean to be a cunt." And suddenly the word "cunt," the ugliest, vilest word, becomes a kind of poetry there for these kids. It's always about the transformative nature of how you turn things upside down or inside out and bring a new meaning. That's the beauty that you strive for.

This poetic beauty is not simply a product of the dialogue itself; it is an effect of the way the dialogue invests itself in the cinematography and the editorial process, which here attains to an extraordinary concision of means, constraining its expressive capacity purely to the motions of the material, to demonstrate its depths by way of a stylistic reduction. It is anything but naïve or amateur, this decision against expression and commentary, but its purpose is to become invisible as a medium.

This is, I will now argue, a type of classicism. From their inception under the auspices of Schiller, Goethe, and the Schlegels in late eighteenth-century Weimar, the principles of modern classicism have been pitted against the emergence and proliferation of the sensations and sentiments associated with romanticism—which is to say, relatively "objective" and dispassionate, wedded to standards of aesthetic harmony and taste that appeal to the enduring, rational qualities of thought and perception, and sheathed in a prophylactic against extremities of feeling that takes the typical mode of irony. Most importantly, classicism vouchsafed a certain division of labor between the *form*—consciously finite, material, and impersonal—and the various *contents*, be they historical, biographical, folkloric, or purely spiritual, given expression in the work; whereas romanticism too often forced a reconciliation between these two distinct moments of the aesthetic, under the sign of enthusiasm, inspiration, or genius, with results that its critics are wont to dismiss as jejune and unearned. As T. S. Eliot once summed up his prejudice in favor of the classical approach to art, "The difference seems to me . . .

34 | **Todd Solondz**

the difference between the complete and the fragmentary, the adult and the immature, the orderly and the chaotic."[27] Yet, despite the imposing instance of so much classicist modernism, the twentieth century managed only fitfully to ward off the appeals of a romanticism it never fully dislodged. From the confessional to the expressionistic, from the Beats to the New Romantics, romanticism survived its disavowal by the cultural commissars of good taste, and its modes proliferated.

One of its bastions of survival was the class of "independent filmmaker," especially in the United States, where Hollywood has typically been depicted as a desert of classical conformity. This prototypical fringe artist-figure, struggling to make ends meet, armed only with amateur equipment, and working with groups of committed acolytes, fulfills all the generic expectations of the type. Is there any more romantic figure in world cinema than Orson Welles, expelled by the system to become its bête noire? Do the reputations of "early" John Cassavetes, David Lynch, Jim Jarmusch, and Todd Haynes hang by any more dependable thread than the presumed authentic rebelliousness implicit in the anti-Hollywood positions they assumed? More important still, however, is the coefficient of those postures in the visual and narrative styles of the films they produced, where every violation of the time-honored rules of continuity editing, single-protagonist story line, professional lighting and sound design, and celebrity casting is a gesture of insubordination and defiance with respect to the overarching industrial conditions of production. "Independent filmmaker" is virtually by definition a romantic job description, with two significant American exceptions—John Sayles and Todd Solondz—each of whom, for different reasons, has tarried with a formal classicism that falls outside the presiding binary opposition.[28]

To clarify this distinct species of classicism, it is crucial to complicate this presiding binary—if not to deconstruct it—between Hollywood and independence. By and large, Solondz is lumped in with other filmmakers—Harmony Korine, Larry Clark, Richard Linklater, and so on—who all fall into what thereby becomes an utterly unwieldy conception of "independent filmmaking," or "smart filmmaking" (in Jeffrey Sconce's memorable phrase), characterized by an "arch emotional nihilism" or some such quality.[29] But this overlooks real formal discrepancies that can perhaps only be mapped by a tactically placed Greimas rectangle.

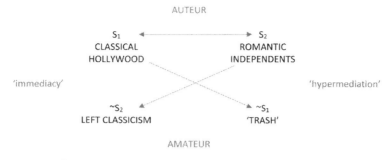

Chart 5. Greimas rectangle: classicism and its others

If Hollywood and so-called independent cinema (e.g., Linklater, Jarmusch, Gus Van Sant) are related along an axis of contrariety, then what I am calling "left classicism" (the so-called neutral term in A. J. Greimas's lexicon) is defined as the contradiction of the contrary term, or "not not-Hollywood" (Solondz, Sayles), while the trash aesthetics of Herschell Gordon Lewis, Mike Kuchar, John Waters, Harmony Korine, and others (the "complex term") is simply a flat contradiction of every stylistic norm of the dominant forces in the industry.[30] There are then relations of implication between the cinema of trash and the "romantic independents" as such, since either category strives for expressive nonidentity with classical commercial cinema, and between "left classicism" and Hollywood, since these categories are associated by strategies of containment and formal "invisibility." Another way of putting this is in the language of media theorists Jay David Bolter and Richard Grusin, who argue that certain media products are "hypermediated" (drawing attention to their status as materially mediated forms), while others are characterized by "immediacy" (seeking to repress or hide their mediation).[31] The semiotic square has the further advantage of positing the two "meta-concepts" generated by its logic: the compound term of the "auteur," who is the complex synthesis of classic Hollywood and independent cinema (Scorsese, Coppola, Lucas, etc.), and the compound term of the "amateur," defined by its being neither left classicism nor trash as such and falling off the grid of commercial viability altogether.

In any event, the square has the specific virtue of identifying the peculiar (and rare) class of Solondz's cinema after *Welcome to the Doll-*

house, emerging out of that film's internalized antagonism between a "romantic independent" sensibility and the mature classicism we have just analyzed in the "first kiss" scene. *Dollhouse* itself, we argued, was a determinate reaction to, and negation of, the aesthetic failure of *Fear, Anxiety, and Depression*, particularly in its relative suppression of "quirkiness" and "neurotic tendencies" at the level of exposition. Thus we can make sense of Solondz's formative stylistic trajectory through its immanent dialectic between the implicit romanticism of all independent US filmmaking and a new kind of classicism that can only be defined through its negation of the negation. I call it "left classicism," since it cannot be said to represent the conservative values and aesthetic protocols of the studio system, while it nevertheless espouses certain principles of form—a modesty of display, a transparency of mediation, and a nonsubjective perspective on the material—that share a good deal with the industry standard.

We now need to come to terms with the exact nature of Solondz's classicism, since it evinces traits and tendencies that are strictly sui generis yet also manages to imply a structural relationship with other classical modes. That it is thoroughly anti-romantic seems unarguable; there are few further gestures in any of his films that indicate the hovering presence of an expressive subjectivity working through and commenting on the material at hand. Instead, the films unfurl in a manner characterized by an inexorable logicality of cause and effect, in an almost mechanical kingdom of consequences, a regime of dour inevitability. (No matter what you do, the pedophile will rape the children; the unwell dog will defecate blood and feces on your floor; the underage girl will pursue an impossible pregnancy through scenes of statutory rape; the exploited domestic servant will murder the affluent family that employs her; the aging, sex-starved barfly will turn the pedophile into a whore.) Classicism tends to prefer a narrative universe of stony fate over a world of contingency mediated by individual will, because the classical worldview is disabused of the myth of individual agency. The father in *Wiener-Dog's* first section tells his son, "Remi, you have to break a dog, break their will, so that they'll submit to your will. It's a kind of civilizing, so they act like humans." Remi asks, "What is a will, exactly?" "It's character, force of character," his father replies. "It's the thing that makes *you*, you." But this force operates *impersonally* in Solondz's world, since there is no question of anybody having any control or agency over their will; rather, that will operates on *them*, submitting them to its pulsions, writing their character in *its* inhuman name. Will is what breaks individuals over its rod.

The monstrosity of will is the bottom line of Solondz's classicism, a terrible shared fatality that manifests in surprising ways, like Aviva's wish for a baby in *Palindromes*. As Lauren Berlant writes, "Her relation to her optimism is to hold on to a phrase and make the world remake itself around it, and when it does not, she finds substitute objects and tries again."[32] There is no choice here, only opportunistic reshufflings of a given, immutable deck. Mark Wiener puts it most forcefully in his monologue at Aviva's welcome-home party near the end of the film:

> People always end up the way they started out. No one ever changes. They think they do, but they don't. If you're the depressed type now, that's the way you'll always be. If you're the mindless happy type now, that's the way you'll be when you grow up. You might lose some weight, your face might clear up, get a body tan, a breast enlargement, a sex change, makes no difference. Essentially, from in front, from behind, whether you're thirteen or fifty, you'll always be the same. . . . There's no free will. I have no choice but to choose what I choose, to do what I do, to live as I live. Ultimately we're all just robots programmed arbitrarily by nature's genetic code. . . . We hope or despair because of the way we've been programmed. Genes and randomness, that's all there is, and none of it matters.

If romanticism posits an infinitely variable self, a limitless, perfectible, self-transcending subjectivity in dialectical compact with its environment, classicism of this "pessimistic" variety seeks to vitiate all such claims at the bar of an entropic physical universe, an absent God, or an irredeemably fallen humanity. What matters is how such a worldview (which is obviously being presented with some irony here: the suspected child molester, who is not a child molester, is providing a defense that he does not require in terms that look like a justification) is elevated to the logic of presentation itself: or how the style of the film, the sum of its technical and formal decisions, underwrites an image of human beings that is as determinist and anti-romantic as this, without abandoning its own audience.

Bear in mind that Hollywood classicism deploys a stylistic strategy of disciplined restraint in order to make a completely contrary case—for the individual as the site of inexhaustible renewal and self-improvement under the rule of capital. In the conventional Hollywood production, obstacles are overcome and divisions bridged so that the protagonist goes through some catalytic transformation and emerges a spiritually improved subject. Nothing could be further from the case of fifteen-year old Aviva in *Palindromes*, who undertakes an extraordinary adventure—engaging in sexual relations with a boy, suffering a coercive abortion and hysterectomy, running away from home, becoming the willing paramour of a trucker, floating alone down a river at night, discovering and joining a community of unwanted children and antiabortion activists, assisting in the assassination of the surgeon who performed her abortion, and watching her accomplice/lover blow his brains out in a cheap motel room—without any transformation whatsoever. Her last line, delivered to the camera, is as good as her first: "I want to have lots and lots of babies, as many babies as possible," becomes "I have a feeling, though it's just a feeling, that this time I'm going to be a mom!" It is the same in *Happiness*, when Billy asks his father if, having raped his school friends Johnny Grasso and Ronald Farber and been arrested for it, he would choose to do it again; the answer is swift and monosyllabic: "Yes." Or the legless, dying Abe Wertheimer in *Dark Horse*, looking up through jaundiced eyes at the woman who has given him fatal hepatitis B and is pregnant with his hated brother's child, with the same quotient of hopeless desire he did in the opening scene. "You spell it backwards or forwards, it stays the same," as Mark Wiener defines "palindrome" for Aviva. "Never changes." The agent of desire, the subject of these films, is in the grip of a will that is *in them more than them*, as Jacques Lacan put it, and it will not allow them to change.[33]

Walter Benjamin once observed of French Classicism's greatest comic exponent, Molière, that he "does not seek to define his creations by the multiplicity of his character traits":

> If the object of psychology is the inner life of man understood empirically, Molière's characters are of no use to it even as a means of demonstration. Character is unfolded in them like a sun, in the brilliance of its single trait, which allows no other to remain visible in its proximity.

The sublimity of character comedy rests on this anonymity of man and his morality, alongside the utmost development of individuality through its exclusive character trait. . . . Complication becomes simplicity, fate freedom. For the character of the comic figure is not the scarecrow of the determinist: it is the beacon in whose beams the freedom of his actions becomes visible. The character trait is . . . the sun of individuality in the colorless (anonymous) sky of man, which casts the shadow of the comic action.[34]

For classicism, this trait, or what Lacan calls *das Ding*, is lodged entirely within the individual while remaining quite external to him, and the resultant comedy of his behavior stems from an all-consuming dedication to what is simultaneously most himself and most destructive to his composure. What Benjamin calls the "anonymity of man" in classical comedy is his wholesale subsumption in "the Thing" of his irredeemably *extimate* drive, which paradoxically leads him to extremes of individuation. If for Molière that "Thing" was miserliness or hypochondria, for Solondz it is pedophilia or teenage motherhood: an exclusive character trait that transmutes into his or her radiance as a person, because it is pursued in the full light of freedom.

The true perversity of Solondz's cinema is the overarching decision to tell *that* kind of story—where nothing really changes and nobody learns anything—in formal terms that resemble the dominant industrial standard. His "left classicism" hijacks many of the conventions of a classical Hollywood production in order to subvert its most sacred underlying presupposition: that the hero is an agent of growth and transformation. In that sense, *Palindromes* is the best single illustration of this aspect of his art, since it pushes to its furthest limit the idea that a "restrained simplicity" of cinematographic and editorial style can be deployed to enframe materials that come openly into conflict with its usual ideological presumptions. Nowhere is that clearer than in the case of the film's casting, but a fuller analysis tells a much more complicated story about style and classicism in relation to extreme materials.

Palindromes is segmented into eight sections (with a brief title-sequence preface), each introduced with a pastel-colored title card that names it and provides a clue to its significance within the whole. This formal decision is already a derailment of any "romantic" expectations

40 | **Todd Solondz**

in the audience, since it shifts the mode of address to something more like a *récit* than a standard narrative voice (which in the commercial cinema almost always decodes into a simple present tense). Lars von Trier has tried this device on several occasions, and its general effect is to institute a significant distance between the narrating instance and the audience, though von Trier goes further still and uses John Hurt as a literal voice-over narrator—in *Dogville* (2003) and *Manderlay* (2005), for instance—to increase the gap. Either way, the consequence of any formal chapterization is a familiar "classicist" separation between form and content, disposing the content in advance as so much known material already categorized, classified, and saturated with irony. The chapter cards—"Dawn," "Judah," "Henry," "Henrietta," "Huckleberry," "Mama Sunshine," "Bob," and "Mark"—all designate characters (or avatars) who are actively or symbolically central to the given episode, directing our attention to certain elements over others. For instance, the two adjacent chapters "Henry" and "Henrietta," refer in name to the aborted fetuses of Joyce Victor (Ellen Barkin), Aviva's mother, and Aviva, respectively. The elevation of these unborn persons to the status of chapter title shows how deeply the eponymous abortees (respectively a brother and a daughter *in potentia*) resonate in Aviva's maternal fantasies—to the extent that she borrows the latter name for herself on the road.

The opening chapter is restrained simplicity itself. An initial "establishing shot" of Aviva's oval portrait on the wall as she cries off-screen and the light switches on is followed by a panning medium shot of Joyce rushing into the room to sit on the bed and embrace her distraught daughter. We then settle into a round of entirely conventional over-the-shoulder shot/reverse-shot edits as they discuss Dawn Wiener's suicide and its implications—twenty shots in total, at an average of six seconds each—with every cut but one tagged to the speech of its framed subject. This is then rounded off with a brief return to the setup of mother and daughter embracing on the bed, and we dissolve to the next title card. There is only one camera movement in the chapter (the early pan), and the frame-ups and edits are conventional to the point of virtual invisibility. Nothing formal in the sequence makes any claim upon the audience's attention, apart from the single conspicuous and unremarked fact that the actors playing mother and daughter are white (Jewish) and African American, respectively. That is to say, the classicism of formal means

The Law of Diminishing Returns | 41

permits an outrage at the level of casting to be perpetrated without any warning or justification or any comment at all. We will return to that elephant in the room shortly.

The chapter titled "Henry" is emotionally the film's most difficult to watch and correspondingly takes more adventurous decisions about framing, movement, and pace of cutting. Although the bulk of this section consists of classically mounted conversations between mother and daughter, those dialogue-driven scenes are sandwiched between shots that accentuate Aviva's growing alienation and isolation within the family—a dramatic reverse tracking shot of mother and daughter exiting the clinic (repeating the device used in *Dollhouse*, when the family leaves the principal's office after the peashooter incident); a graceful reverse dolly of the composition book in which Aviva is listing possible names for her baby; a left-lateral tracking shot of the exterior of the house that cuts to a right-dollying close-up of Aviva in her room "feeding" a baby doll; a particularly punishing long take of Aviva, at medium distance, huddled on her bed, recoiling from her father's violent attempt on her door (more on this later); another slowly reversing dolly of Aviva on the operating table at the abortion clinic; and three out-of-focus point-of-view shots of her, in recovery, overhearing snippets of bad news about the procedure, dissolving in and out of bright white light (and featuring heavy distortion and echo on the soundtrack). These much more expressive cinematic gestures tie intimately to the evolving material and wean the audience away from the fixed idea that home is the safest place for Aviva to be. They pry the film out of the moral conventionality in which the situation seems rooted and establish plausible grounds for sympathizing with Aviva's aberrant wishes. All of this is exquisitely amplified on the soundtrack by the film's first use of the haunting lullaby theme written for Aviva by Nathan Larson and sung by Nina Persson: a simple minor-key melodic rise and fall in 3/4 time, set against piano, synthesized strings, and a subtle electric guitar and bass. The theme sutures us into Aviva's growing misery with effortless ease, as a lullaby soothes a crying child.

The film's first use of extreme satiric irony takes place in the "Henrietta" chapter, when "Joe" the trucker mounts and then sodomizes Aviva in the Budget 19 motel, and this sudden shift into grubby statutory rape (from the implicit romance of the road) is accompanied on the

42 | **Todd Solondz**

soundtrack by the elegant sounds of Tchaikovsky's first Piano Concerto in B-flat Major. What Aviva hears during her second sexual encounter are the stirring strains of late-romantic ecstasy, while what we see, in a steady, nonjudgmental backward dolly, is a workingman's opportunist anal rape of a runaway minor. "Can you still get pregnant [*grunt*] when it goes in there?," she asks hopefully as the scene fades to white. Here, then, the film has pulled back away from an intense identification with its heroine and presented her self-destructive naïveté and *idée fixe* in a more objective manner, as a disease of her perceptions. But this works the more forcefully because of the unwonted degree of proximity attained in the "Henry" chapter. Form in the medium of film is a matter of arranging blocks of moving images in such a way that their succession is felt as more than additive, more than simply incremental. It is the *product*, not the sum, of carefully calibrated differentials of mood and tone in the sequence of scenes. The tonal distance achieved here is felt again in the "morning after" scene when, following a desultory conversation with the obviously embarrassed and fleeing "Joe," Aviva prepares to meet him in the coffee shop. A rapid-fire montage of upbeat shots of her smiling in the shower, and a couple of handheld traveling shots of her exiting the motel room and hurrying to her appointment, is set to a particularly chirpy, daytime-TV musical theme exuding adolescent optimism, which breaks off suddenly into silence as Aviva confronts the CLOSED sign in the door to the café and wheels around bewildered. Her total abandonment is then captured in a high-angle long shot of her tiny body standing alone in the empty parking lot outside the shuttered diner. The chapter thus closes on a note that further "objectifies" Aviva, presenting her as the victim of her own misconceptions and optimism.

It is here that we segue into the most magical sequence of filmmaking in Solondz's career, a chapter titled "Huckleberry" that works as a formal pivot away from realism and into much more fantastical territory. Its brief, two-minute duration, set entirely to Larson's "Lullaby" theme, concerns Aviva's solitary drift away from all known coordinates. "I knew I had to in a sense 'go down the rabbit hole,'" remarks Solondz in our interview, "and I needed something that could bring me there, that could express moving into another kind of reality." His solution was both elegantly simple and (in the context of his body of work) exceptionally audacious. For rather than persevere stylistically in the vein already established, or joining seamlessly with the memorably over-the-top sequence to follow ("Mama Sunshine"), the studiously restrained director has opted to indulge in the most luridly cinematic homage of his career: an achingly beautiful paean to Charles Laughton's *The Night of the Hunter* (1955)—specifically, the otherworldly sequence of the children's nocturnal escape downriver. Aviva walks forlornly away from the road, through paddock and pasture, over hill and down dale, dragging her wheelie carry-on case behind her as flocks of sheep graze, crops quiver in the breeze, and the setting sun etches a silhouette of our lone heroine against a massing, grandiloquent sky. Arriving at the inevitable riverbed at dusk, she finds waiting for her a child's plastic toy boat, just large enough to accommodate her exhausted body, and as she drifts oblivious into the night, a tiny lamb nibbles daintily at the bank.

This self-contained vignette, as poignant as it is gorgeous, serves as a kind of vent for the accumulating background pressures of Solondz's cinephilia, which his left classicism has effectively banished from expression in the foreground of his work. Here, *in nuce*, are all the disavowed tendencies toward independent romanticism that his prevailing austerity has displaced onto this relatively autonomous, and separable, two-minute sequence. "Huckleberry" is high art cinema in minutiae, oozing with visual style; each shot feels almost European in its compositional elegance

Figure 7. *Palindromes* (2004): the "Huckleberry" sequence

and symmetry, and their rhythmic synthesis into a dynamic image of late afternoon and evening evokes a high romantic melancholia. Above all, the homage to Laughton opens a vein of auteurist sensibility, where the "post-cinematic" wasteland of 2004 is suddenly irradiated with the lost aesthetic grandeur of one of world cinema's greatest years, 1955—year of *Ordet* (Carl Theodor Dreyer, Denmark), *Smiles of a Summer Night* (Ingmar Bergman, Sweden), *Pather Panchali* (Satyajit Ray, India), *All That Heaven Allows* (Douglas Sirk, US), *Moonfleet* (Fritz Lang, US), *Lola Montès* (Max Ophuls, France), *Night and Fog* (Alain Resnais, France), and, of course, *The Night of the Hunter*.

Laughton's film also provides the key to the best-remembered chapter of *Palindromes*, set in the rural retreat of Mama Sunshine and her adopted family of misfits and unwanted children. This unlikely utopia is an expanded version of Mrs. Cooper's (Lillian Gish's) house in Laughton's classic, and her ragged passel of orphaned kids raised by Christian love and charity against all odds in a brutal Depression-era United States. But it is also a mediated version of one of Solondz's best-loved films of early childhood, *The Sound of Music* (Robert Wise, 1965), which motivates the device of the Sunshine Singers' performances of "Nobody Jesus but You" and "Fight for the Children." Every element of this chapter is tonally exaggerated and bathed in the glow of irreality, from Peter Paul's enthusiastic enunciations of "Jesus Tears!" and "He's the nicest!," to Mama Sunshine's angelic mien, to Barbara's dispassionate account of being raised by an abusive drug addict, to the perfect circle of damage, disadvantage, and disability described by the children themselves around the breakfast table—Barbara is a blind albino; Jiminy is presumably gay; Crystal is missing both arms; Skippy has severe Down syndrome; Shazaam has badly crippled legs; Trixie is a dwarf; Ali was "born a heathen," as Peter Paul points out, "but he's been saved"; Ell has leukemia; Carlito is an epileptic; and Peter Paul himself has to clear the mucus from his lungs before he sleeps. Each is an emanation, a "might have been," rescued, as it were, from the rancid garbage heap to which Peter Paul takes Aviva on a pilgrimage of horror: "where they throw out unborn babies. See, every so often, a truck comes by from some baby killers and dumps this stuff." So each Sunshine child inhabits the world at an obtuse angle to its reality principle, in the sunny lap of Jesus Christ, redeemed from the abortive slime that Peter Paul holds up for

Dawn's inspection in a sealed plastic baggie. To that extent, of course, the entire sequence is a wish fulfillment of Dawn's fevered dream work, desperately trying to undo the damage done to her and to Henrietta—the terminated fetus whose name she has adopted—by the same Dr. Fleischer she will end up helping to assassinate in the next chapter, in a quid pro quo exchange of fatalities. This is the bottom of the rabbit hole, where our latter-day Alice discovers her fantasies walking the earth in three dimensions, and here, as in Lewis Carroll, the humor is alarming. Of all the outrageous gags in the chapter, I will quote only one: Mama Sunshine's weepy regret that "last year our special daughter, Nardika, ran away, and she didn't even have any legs."

For all that tonal excess, however, the style of cinematic narration in this chapter is conservative, as if having cast us down the rabbit hole in "Huckleberry," Solondz was determined that its far end should return us to familiar ground. Shot/reverse-shot dialogue scenes, basic establishment shots, invisible "motivated" cutting between medium shots and close-ups in the performance sequences, eye-line matches, simple descriptive pans, and so forth; there is even a structural repeat of the mother-daughter exchange on a bed from the first chapter. It is as if after all the visual pleasure of the previous chapter, and the vocal shift from subjectivity to objectivity that distinguishes "Henry" from "Henrietta," Solondz wanted to regroup and establish a base of stylistic operations on the film's home territory. The more outlandish the material, the more classical his narration becomes, in a pattern of compensation that can now be clearly discerned. It is exactly as he puts it: restrained simplicity governs the cinematic style to the extent that "there is [already] so much of a charge in the material." Left classicism is not about accentuating the perversity or extremity of the materials; it is not about amplifying or finding a requisite idiom for the given "charge." It is instead about stripping away any tendentiously expressive gesture in order that the material stand exposed in all of its terrible awkwardness.

Of course, we have not yet mentioned this chapter's most outlandish formal element: the casting of Aviva as a fully grown, obese, African American woman (Sharon Wilkins), who fits into the striped tank top and low-slung denim jeans of Aviva's running-away outfit with all the surreal grace of Vladimir Mayakovsky's "cloud in pants" and whose light flirtations with the ten-year-old Peter Paul begin to feel sickening. It

46 | **Todd Solondz**

now behooves us to come to terms with this, the film's most extraordinary structural feature: that each chapter casts a different performer in the lead role, eight actors related not by resemblance but by the very disjunction of their respective appearances. While our initial Aviva ("Dawn's" Emani Sledge) is a prepubescent African American girl who fits speculatively into the role of only child to a middle-class family of Jewish New Jersey suburbanites, the next actor in the role (Valerie Shusterov, of "Judah") is at least appropriately Jewish-looking, with medium-length dark curly hair and dark brown eyes, and plump enough to make a natural fit with her spur-of-the-moment lover, Judah (Robert Agri). But the transition to the "Henry" Aviva (Hannah Freiman) means we must transfer our empathies to a gangly, freckle-faced, braces-wearing, redheaded adolescent with no weight issues to speak of, yet in whom (as we have seen) the film style asks that we make exceptional affective investments. The Aviva of "Henrietta" (Rachel Corr), meanwhile, seems like a reversion to the physical type of the "Judah" Aviva, only slimmer and just enough younger to make the statutory rape scene extremely unpleasant. This is followed by the truly confounding casting of a boy, Will Denton, as the "Huckleberry" Aviva, both as a nod to Mark Twain's eponymous hero and to undermine all of our remaining expectations, of which there had been few enough. Thus, Sharon Wilkins's "Mama Sunshine" Aviva is something like the summa of all these disappointments, these repeated shocks of realignment and unwonted adjustment, since she so manifestly does not "fit" even the blurry, composite outline of Aviva that we have hesitantly pieced together out of the available evidence to this point. With this, all bets are off, and the subsequent shifts—to the reassuringly plausible Shayna Levine for the climactic "Bob" chapter and the disreputably implausible Jennifer Jason Leigh (age forty-two at the time of filming) for the epilogue, "Mark"—simply underscore the point made so abundantly already.

Cinema has, of course, often had recourse to the device of casting multiple actors in a single role, particularly to cover a larger range of diegetic years than usual, and especially to cast infant and child actors in the role of a character who subsequently matures. Biopics frequently avail themselves of this efficiency, and epics (like the *Star Wars* saga or *The Godfather* trilogy), given their sprawling time schemes, also sometimes cast two or more actors in the central roles. (Darth Vader, or

Anakin Skywalker, for instance, is variously played by David Prowse, James Earl Jones, Hayden Christensen, Gene Bryant, Spenser Wilding, Ben Burtt, Jake Lloyd, Sebastian Shaw, and others.) In certain franchises whose longevity outstrips the professional careers or even life spans of given actors, various performers—like those who have played James Bond or Dr. Who—are slotted into the role with more or less audience approval. But in such cases there is the tacit understanding (or the written justification) that the obvious physical differences between these actors should be politely overlooked, that our "willing suspension of disbelief" be particularly applied to these visible seams in the narrative fabric out of a sense of solidarity with the aims of the production. In his glorious "Apu" trilogy, Satyajit Ray exploited the one- and three-year gaps between the films' productions, and the substantial diegetic age gaps between the title character's featured phase of life in each film (childhood, college days, and married parenthood), to paper over viewers' inevitable sense of disorientation as we follow Apu's life story. Meanwhile, Coppola's decision to follow his depiction of the aged Don Corleone (Marlon Brando) in *The Godfather* with sequences from his early life in America as the dashing young Vito (Robert De Niro) two years later in the sequel could be said to be doubly motivated by the shifting tectonics of Hollywood star power in the 1970s (finding a charismatic "equivalent" for the declining Brando) and by the need to compensate for the older star's refusal to appear in the second installment. In a far more conventional example, Ang Lee's *Hulk* (2003), one actor is used to play Bruce Banner as a baby, another to play him as a teenager, and a third—the star, Eric Bana—as an adult, while a series of algorithms is deployed to present his fourth screen incarnation, the Hulk. The audience is manipulated to see continuity where the eye sees difference, often through the covert application of special makeup and CGI effects. Barry Jenkins's *Moonlight* (2016), on the other hand, uses its tripartite structure, and the several diegetic years that pass between each chapter, to justify the casting in the lead role of three actors who resemble one another not at all.

None of this, however, applies to Solondz's intentions in *Palindromes*, which, in casting eight actors of entirely different ages, colors, sexes, and sizes in the role of a character who ages approximately ten weeks over the course of the last seven chapters of the film, violates every rule of continuity and plausibility established by the commercial narrative film industry—in America or elsewhere. The only US film that comes close to touching its radical agenda in casting is one that explicitly followed its example: Todd Haynes's Bob Dylan-ish biopic *I'm Not There*, which cast six actors (including one female, one black and underage) in the role of the mythical Dylan figure, in chapters that diverge strongly in style and tone among themselves.[35] Solondz's extreme casting in *Palindromes* ranks among the medium's most disconcerting strategies of ostensibly Brechtian *Verfremdung*—though Bertolt Brecht himself never went so far in thirty-seven years of work for the stage. In some ways the most obvious screen precedent is the logical inverse of the device: Alec Guinness playing all nine members of the D'Ascoyne family in *Kind Hearts and Coronets* (Robert Hamer, 1949), or Peter Sellers performing three entirely different characters in *Dr. Strangelove, or: How I Learned to Stop Worrying and Love the Bomb* (Stanley Kubrick, 1964), though such a trick is ultimately more about star versatility and range than audience estrangement. It is my sense that perhaps one peculiar development in the contemporary cinema may have spurred Solondz's radicalism here, and that was the opening movement of David Lynch's "fugue state" trilogy, *Lost Highway* (1998), where the extraordinary sense that Balthazar Getty and Bill Pullman were, after all, playing different aspects of the same person came as that film's chief formal scandal and made a significant adjustment to the very meaning of film characterization at the time. Nevertheless, the extreme evolution forced on this formal mutation by Solondz in 2004's *Palindromes* stands alone for its boldness and uncompromising refusal to explain. Unlike Lynch's film, no other character seems to notice any difference in Aviva's appearance, and unlike Haynes's, one does not have the structural justification of an apparent omnibus production of "the many different Bob Dylans," all shot in different styles, to explain the constant changes.

The preeminent effect of this device is a thorough dismantlement of the very idea of star power at the point—the central character, present in every scene—where one is most primed to expect its appearance. For not only is each of the seven actors who take us up to the final chapter an "unknown" in industry terms—an actor with no portfolio to speak of at the time of filming and who has not managed to build one since—but none of them is able to discover in the role

The Law of Diminishing Returns | 49

the conditions for a "breakout" performance in the first place. On the contrary, deprived of any opportunity to construct a balanced screen presence against the film's only named property, Ellen Barkin, by virtue of their character's singular immaturity, the actors then face: (1) the cramped limits of the chapterized structure of the film, according to which none of them has more than fifteen minutes of screen time, and (2) Solondz's chafing performance direction, dictating that Aviva's voice should never rise above a timid simper or whimper and that her body language should be as self-effacing as possible. The character has no speeches to make, she learns nothing in the course of the film, and what fascination there is on the screen never belongs to her as a figure. There is thus not a chance that Aviva should offer any of these actors a vessel for aspirations toward stardom, since she is a black hole of charisma who—unlike Dawn Wiener for Heather Matarazzo, as a counterexample, or Scooby Livingston for Mark Webber—hasn't even the appeal of an underdog personality to channel our affections. We will see this same structure of feeling reinvented for the central character of Solondz's "rom com," *Dark Horse*,[36] but here the point is starkly raised that *Palindromes* has at its center something like cinematic antimatter—ordinary-looking people with no name, and very little talent, performing within strictly delimited parameters a role it is virtually impossible to admire. It is as if the entire film consisted of an edited series of clips taken from an eternal casting session, open to the whole world, for a role that will never be filled, because nobody will want to watch it. This is why the casting of Jennifer Jason Leigh in the final chapter is the exception that clinches the rule, for by this stage—given that Leigh (an exceptionally talented and versatile actor, who for years had wanted to work for Solondz) is obliged to play Aviva with the very same narrow range of tones and mannerisms the string of nonprofessionals has struggled with—the point is already abundantly clear: Aviva is the neutralization and cancelation of star power per se. She is where screen glamour goes to die.

The purpose of Solondz's relentlessly circumscribed style is thus not to suture our identification to his central character (apart from some exceptional moments), but to create a sequence of subtly varying tone colors, chapter to chapter, whose overall effect is the foreclosure of interpretive intentionality in favor of a logical consistency of movement.

50 | **Todd Solondz**

Table 2. *Palindromes* structures

AVIVA	CASTING	PRESENTATION	MOOD
"Dawn"	Prepubescent African American girl	Objective, dialogue	Insulation
"Judah"	Pubescent Jewish girl	Objective, encounter	Objectification
"Henry"	Pubescent goy girl	Subjective, alienation	Interiority
"Henrietta"	Pubescent Jewish girl	Objective, satire	Discordance
"Huckleberry"	Pubescent goy boy	Subjective, romance	Expression
"Mama Sunshine"	Obese fully grown African American woman	Objective, parody	Exaggeration
"Bob"	Pubescent Jewish girl	Objective, action	Kinetic explosion
"Mark"	Middle-aged Jewish woman "star"	Objective, dialogue	Recoil

In this context, it matters far less "who" Aviva is—and what she looks like—than the place she occupies in an evolving schema of cinematic moods, dictated at the upper limit by a resolute sense of formal closure. Such, in fact, is the underlying truth of all classical productions, which are synthesized artificially out of working narrative fragments pegged to a preconceived template of modal fall and rise, dislocation and reassociation. Only here the fundamental glue of audience identification—the casting of the central role—is keyed to very different aspects of the shifting modal language games than that of characterological consistency. The scandalous decision about casting gives the lie to the ideological coherence of the form itself and obliges us to come to very different terms with what a classical construction *is* and how it works.

At the same time, the film makes the case that, *even so*—despite all that radical deconstruction of narrative cinema's characterization—Aviva is perfectly legible as a figure of persistence from chapter to chapter. The grammar of the form compels a continuity that the eye and ear disavow in the act of recognizing it. Because the chapters merge technically under the formal processes of shot/reverse-shot editing, eye-line matches, balanced compositions, motivated camera movements, and so forth—because their aesthetic differences are confined to the *tonal* register rather than the underlying *stylistic* one—there is nothing to prevent our cinematic unconscious from performing the involuntary suture that identifies "obese African American woman" with "pubescent white boy" under the flexible, composite rubric of the name, the performance style, and the simple lines of dialogue that define "Aviva" as a character. Classicism is thus a way, at least in this high-risk "left" variant of it, of having one's cake and eating it, too, since it both legislates an automatism of the various narrative functions and displays their perfect conventionality and artificiality at one and the same time.

Eternally Diminishing Returns

It took a precocious classical philologist, who subsequently went through a dramatic romantic swerve (Wagner worship, the Dionysian revolt), to affirm in modern accents perhaps classicism's most formidable concept: eternal recurrence. First flirted with in Nietzsche's *The Gay Science* (1882) and then propounded as a doctrine in his highly literary *Thus Spake Zarathustra* (1891), this idea—patched together out of dozens of disparate sources, ancient and modern—is pivotal to the progress of modern thought and to the cinema of Todd Solondz. As his menagerie of animals points out to the hermit-prophet Zarathustra:

> "Behold, we know what you teach: that all things recur eternally and we ourselves with them, and that we have already existed an infinite number of times before and all things with us. You teach that there is a great year of becoming, a colossus of a year: this year must, like an hourglass, turn itself over again and again, so that it may run down and run out anew: So that all these years resemble one another, in the greatest things and in the smallest, so that we ourselves resemble ourselves in each great year, in the greatest things and in the smallest."[37]

And they imagine Zarathustra's response to his own impending death:

> "'But the complex of causes in which I am entangled will recur—it will create me again! I myself am part of these causes of the eternal recurrence. I shall return, with this sun, with this earth, with this eagle, with this serpent—*not* to a new life or a better life or a similar life: I shall return eternally to this identical and self-same life, in the greatest things and in the smallest.'"[38]

The point of Zarathustra's imposing doctrine on the "flat circle" of time, in which nothing will ever truly change from the viewpoint of eternity, is, however, a residually romantic affirmation: not to despair of the meaninglessness of such inevitable repetitions but precisely to *will* them as such, to align one's desire with the exact contours of one's fate, in the full knowledge that they will never cease to be re-occasioned, and oneself in their midst. Nietzsche calls this desired palindromic reversibility *amor fati*: "That one wants nothing to be different, not forward, not backward, not in all eternity. Not merely bear what is necessary, still less conceal it . . . but love it."[39]

In the context of our ongoing discussion of Solondz's work, we can now begin to see points of both convergence and divergence with this postulate. On the one hand, as we are about to see in much more detail, we can make out a profound sympathy with the notion of irresistible recurrence as various patterns, thematics, and personae seem to be endlessly resurrected and restated across the body of work. As well, we gradually piece together irrefutable evidence of a closed cinematic universe embroiled in a well-nigh cosmic cyclicity of temporal and material functions across a limited number of variables. On the other hand, however, we note the absence of this last affirmative note in Nietzsche's morality, since, as we have been suggesting from the start, what we bear witness to in this body of work is a *law of diminishing returns* such that each repetition is just that little bit worse, a little grayer and less compelling, than the last, leaving us in a situation where it is virtually impossible to espouse the proposed *amor fati*. Rather, a profound melancholy radiates from the core nodes of recurrence in this cinema; to come back is always to feel the relentless drudgery of going through those same motions again, to no greater purpose and with no greater wisdom than in the last iteration of this prison house of destiny. Think only of Consuelo, whose earlier avatar we meet briefly in *Happiness* on hands and knees and in marigolds, sweating over a bucket on the tiled floor, in our first introduction to the Maplewood house, and who has been expanded into an entire United Colors of Benetton staff at Helen Jordan's villa in *Life During Wartime* (black concierge, Asian chef, etc.). Color, class, and ethnicity are destiny in an absolute sense here, and the serial repetitions of mindless, thankless toil offer no solace and nothing worth affirming. Nietzsche never meant his *amor fati* for the proletariat, to be sure, but Solondz's films take seriously the prospect of a universe of eternal return for the people whose suffering and misery provide a constant foil for the joyous affirmations of the rare "blonde beasts" (whom we never meet here either). The name of that universe is, of course, *capitalism*, in which there is no "great year of becoming" looming on the calendar, no sublime jubilee to look ahead to, just more and more of the same stuff, only slightly cheaper and less fulfilling. In order to make sense of Solondz's map of this plane of immanence, however, we need to be clear about its key.

Take a character called Jiminy, played in three films by Tyler Maynard. His place at the helm of the Sunshine Singers in *Palindromes* was assured by his choreographic flair and dazzling smile; we had assumed that his "affliction" in the eyes of Jesus was homosexuality but only on the basis of the campy excess of his antiabortion performances. And given the somewhat fantastical cast of that section of the film, frankly we had been in some doubt as to the categorical nature of his existence, placed, as he was, at several degrees of separation from the reality principle. Yet we find him again in *Dark Horse*, now thoroughly absorbed into the apparatus of late capitalism as a store clerk in the complaints department of a barn-size Toys"R"Us franchise in Livingston, New Jersey. This Jiminy is every bit as amiable as the Jiminy of Mama Sunshine, but that incandescent niceness has been subsumed into the creation of value for a large corporate chain, and it decodes as the kind of wretchedly inauthentic "affective labor" that incites homicidal tendencies. We meet him twice in the film, once in a "realistic" confrontation, when Abe comes to return a scratched *Lord of the Rings* action figure, and later in a dream sequence, when Abe is looking to reclaim his misplaced fiancée. The sympathetic wincing and grimacing Jiminy uses to accompany his mandated refusal to refund the child's toy is all too familiar in our age of "immaterial labor," when these targeted gestures of care and concern are specifically exploited as a source of augmented brand value. His unflappable, low-toned, oh-so-polite resistance to every one of Abe's lines of attack results in the latter's inevitable explosion: "I have no time for this shit! You'll be hearing from my attorney!" In roughly forty seconds, we have experienced both the satisfying return of Jiminy, his transplantation from one film into another, and the terribly unsatisfying traducement of his personal charm, its transformation into a corporate façade. So it is toward the end of the film, when Abe's unconscious reaches for a satisfactory Kafkaesque mask to affix to his inability to succeed at anything, that Jiminy's is the face it finds. As his comatose mind appeals, desperately, against the cruel fate that has landed him legless in hospital with hepatitis B, Abe once again comes face-to-face with the sunny, unyielding visage of the Toys"R"Us customer service clerk and his syrupy corporate rhetoric:

> "Oh, hi! Can I help you? . . . I'm sorry, we don't carry any fiancées here. . . . Maybe you'd like to try one of our other outlets? . . . Sorry, [the store manager's] out for lunch, but he'll be back in a few minutes, if you'd like to wait. . . . Maybe you'd like to flip through our catalog. We could special order for you, if you'd like. But I'm afraid, once a purchase has been opened, it can't be returned. Store policy. . . . I'm sorry, but I'm afraid I can't make out the date [on the receipt]. . . . I'm sorry, but this was a final sale. . . . Sorry."

Five times the pleasant face says it is "sorry," twice it pads bad news with an "I'm afraid," and four times it offers alternatives with the conditional subjunctive of "if you'd like." There is not the glimmer of an actual soul underneath these shopworn clichés. Jiminy is a puppet of the rhetoric that speaks through him.

The gatekeeper character appears again in *Wiener-Dog*, this time as a transgendered *acousmêtre* whom we overhear on Dave Schmerz's calls to his agent's office, and once again she is a mere appendage to the language that animates her vocal cords: "I'm so sorry. . . . Well, he's been, like, crazy busy these last few weeks? The whole agency's doing this radical reshuffle? Oh, wait, I think he's just wrapping up his FaceTime. Let me see if I can pull some magic!" Just as in *Dark Horse*, Jiminy is the "outer office" barrier, the ward who keeps the protagonist apart from the donor figure (store manager, agent) and frustrates narrative progress. Her decline from the callisthenic antics of *Palindromes* to this unseen functionary of a faceless corporate system is complete; all of her native spark and charisma has been liquidated and applied as immaterial lubricant to the wheels of commercial exploitation.

Eternal recurrence is thus put through the mangler of a core economic principle: the law of diminishing returns. What begins as the incarnation of a certain kind of promise or value turns out in the next iteration to be reduced, degraded in stature or quality. Take the instance of Vi (Selma Blair), the central character in Solondz's most brutal anecdote, the opening segment of *Storytelling*, titled "Fiction." Vi is a prototypical white liberal BFA sophomore, wearing her "Biko Lives" tee, fucking the classmate with cerebral palsy because she thinks he might be different, the inevitable pro-choice and "politics of prisoners" posters Blu-Tacked to the walls of her dorm room. Yet, what happens to her has a pseudo-transformative power: not that it forces any conspicuous moral growth or obvious learning curve, but her rape at the hands of her uncompromisingly critical professor (to which she only appears to consent due to a determination not to "be racist," a knee-jerk white guilt that has her repeatedly shouting out "Nigger, fuck me harder!" on his exact instructions) at least wrings from her a *histoire-à-clef* that might, with enough reflection, become a true experience. We take leave of her in a seething rage, brutalized by both the class authority figure and the assorted judgments of the other students, trying to reassemble the pieces of her fractured being. It is not the most auspicious of transformations, but this raw exposure to the implications of the assumptions underlying her hitherto privileged existence has at least clarified a possible trajectory away from that life.

The next time we meet her, however, ten years later in *Dark Horse*, it is as if nothing has changed other than her aging body and her name. Now called Miranda, she lives at home with her parents in a suburban house, her Ikea bookcases still crowded with college textbooks, stacks of notebooks on her desk, naïve sketches and ribbons pinned to a corkboard, an "AIDS WALK" poster on the wall, and a dream catcher hooked over the head of her single bed—there is nothing here to suggest any growth at all. She does carry the hepatitis B virus, however, a fact she neglects to share with her suitor, Abe Wertheimer, before sharing her toothbrush, and her moral dilemma in this film boils down to whether she should terminate her protracted adolescence with a wedding to the only person who approaches her with unalloyed love. "I *want* to want you," she sighs to Abe. "I had a long Skype with Mahmoud, my ex, and I told him all about you. How different you are from what I'm used to. All the downside, everything. And he agrees: I should stop trying to slit my wrists, give up on a literary career, give up on hope, ambition, success, independence, self-respect. I should just get married and have children." All the overt comedy here is subtly modified by our lingering knowledge that, already ten years before, her teacher Mr. Scott had told her she had no talent and should stop writing, that persisting in a "literary career" was a pipe dream, a judgment made good by his violent rape of her body and her principles, so that this belated advice by another "colored" authority figure feels like another twist in the tail of the same eternal recurrence, into which Abe erupts as a portly Messiah, an actual event. But making a purse out of this sow's ear proves impossible after all, and in the cruel denouement, Miranda has transferred her attentions to Abe's far more successful and better-looking brother, a surgeon, and bears his child to Abe's funeral. The ten years that have lapsed between "Vi's" rape and "Miranda's" final abandonment of all ambition, independence, and self-respect have thus ripened nothing, no true experience or moral chrysalis, out of the ruins of her student years. The character's return is a repeat, with fewer options. Such is the law of diminishing returns.

Of course, the major type of pattern repetition in Solondz's work concerns the larger familial structures: the Wieners, Jordans, and Maplewoods who married into the latter clan. To examine this aspect of the auteur's concern with eternally diminishing recurrences is simultaneously to disclose his developing interest in authorial "world creation," à la Balzac in the *Comédie humaine* and William Faulkner's Yoknapatawpha cycle. Solondz's larger familial networks, Jewish on the whole and based genetically in New Jersey, open up broader horizons than the suburban home as such and touch, too, on longer temporal dimensions. So the unhappy elder Jordan couple in *Happiness*, Mona and Lenny (Louise Lasser and Ben Gazzara), have already retired to Florida in that film, where they promptly separate, a move that entails holiday travel for the rest of the family and so precipitates a more comprehensive scattering in the pseudo-sequel, *Life During Wartime*, where only Joy has remained faithful to the Jersey (thus liberal, cosmopolitan) lifestyle. Trish has decamped with her own children to Florida after her divorce from their pedophile father and there seeks resettlement with a "normal" Jewish divorcé and Jersey exile, Harvey Wiener. And Helen has extracted herself from the network altogether, seeking an upscale refuge from the incorrigibly middle-class philistinism of the Jordan clan. These contingencies of the familial web stretch narrative time and space even as they stitch the cinematic chronotope back together again on a wider set of coordinates. And such correspondences with Faulkner's Snopeses, Compsons, and Sartorises, not to mention the networks extending around Balzac's Rastignac, Lucien Chardon, and Vautrin, suggest that here Solondz is thinking in a more distributed manner than in most art house cinema. To be sure, there are more pertinent touchstones than these giants of the literary world, and while Solondz himself likes to mention the *Star Wars* and *Star Trek* cycles as ironic comparisons to his world-building enterprise, perhaps the most relevant point of reference is the daytime soaps and sitcoms (with their spin-offs) that so many of his setups come to resemble—a subject that is further discussed below.

But what matters in the extension of this more distributed characterological system is precisely the opportunities it affords for "diminishing returns" along the lines already sketched here. It is not merely that these characters recur from film to film; it is that when they do, they are inevitably sapped of some of their earlier allure and fascination, "worsened" and degraded by a law that prevails over Solondz's oeuvre. Once again, much of this hinges on casting, as we shall see, but not all of it, and in turning to consider *Life During Wartime* in some depth in what follows, our concern is, above all, with the congeries of formal and technical decisions that militates against a rehabilitation of the specific charms and attractions of *Happiness* (of which it is a sequel in narrative terms only) while, stylistically, terms like "dimming" and "disappointment" seem more appropriate. There are precedents for this deliberate downgrading of the pleasures associated with an earlier, more successful film in its sequel. The most striking and illuminating of these is probably Wong Kar-Wai's decision to use his sci-fi movie *2046* (2004) as a kind of programmatic negation of all the fetishistic cinematic values accruing to the luminous work to which it is a sequel of sorts, *In the Mood for Love* (2000), if it is not David Lynch's savage denunciation of his TV fan base in the extraordinarily intemperate film spin-off prequel, *Twin Peaks: Fire Walk with Me* (1992). Placing *Life During Wartime* in this company is not meant to do anything other than associate it with a determinate auteurist strategy: the hijacking of an existing cinematic allure in the interests of sabotaging what it has come to represent to the maker and to us. If I now make the claim that *Happiness* has every right to be considered Solondz's masterpiece, it rapidly becomes apparent why

58 | **Todd Solondz**

its author, having been able to produce only two other films in the ten years following its release (with exponentially depreciating fortunes), should want to return to the last of his works that actually managed to "break even" and exact a peculiar kind of aesthetic revenge on its status and artistic halo.

Opening with the same sprightly Robbie Kondor violin theme from the earlier *chef d'oeuvre*, played over title cards inscribed in identical, flowing white calligraphy on elegantly framed sable grounds, *Life During Wartime* explicitly enacts a logic of repetition that its first scene indulges to an uncanny extent. The initial shot of either film is a five-second close-up of Joy Jordan, against that same florid restaurant banquette and embowered in a lavish floral arrangement, looking anxiously off-screen to her dinner partner, to whom we cut in another emotionally charged close-up, four seconds long, before cutting back to Joy. This extraordinary synchronicity, which can be tracked over a longer duration by playing the two scenes simultaneously, has very few precedents in world cinema and was insisted upon by the filmmaker. As cinematographer Ed Lachman recalls, "He wanted to recreate the first scene [of *Happiness*], which I found really compelling, so we actually tried to be true to how the first scene was: like the back of the banquette where they're sitting at the restaurant, and the flowers; so, I just tried to be true in recreating the style and the look."[40] There are significant divergences, to be sure, and we will turn to those in a minute, but the frame-ups and almost nonexistent camera movements, the focal depths of each shot, the side lighting and chiaroscuro facial salience, the editorial rhythm to and fro, the specific contents of some of the dialogue, the intonation of the actors' voices, the costumes (the man's suit has changed fabric, but Joy's crochet vest is the same, albeit worn over a blouse in the sequel), the décor, the props (an identical gold-inlay-based pewter porringer inscribed "JOY," the same wine glasses filled with water, similar table candles in fishbowls—only the glass ashtray has been removed, tacitly reflecting the altered laws on smoking in restaurants in the ten-year gap between these scenes)—all participate in a logic of repetition that fully encourages us to nod in sympathy with Joy's disclaimer that she's feeling fine, "just a little déjà vu."

Soon enough, however, the discrepancies begin to announce themselves. We'll attend to the casting shortly, but even apart from that, sig-

The Law of Diminishing Returns | 59

Figure 8. *Happiness* (1998) and *Life During Wartime* (2009): the Gansevoort reproduction

nificant differences are obvious. First, the lighting and color palette are distinctly moodier and darker in the opening of the sequel than in the original. Whereas *Happiness* went for a pink and white palette, playing off Jane Adams's ivory-pale skin and blush tones, the repeat is suffused in an otherworldly golden glow, almost as if the flush of sunset had been cast over the dim restaurant interior. Lachman has spoken of wanting to establish continuity with the warmth of the rest of the film's Florida setting (and lighting), but there is something decidedly non-naturalistic about this heat-lamp glow, which glazes the actors in an oneiric gel. The luminosity is more targeted as well, squeezing the broad spectrum of *Happiness'* subtle highlights and multitudinous shadows into a more bifurcated chiaroscuro; thus, the anonymous, out-of-focus background of a popular restaurant at peak hour is blackened out in a thick atmosphere of darkness as all our attention is trained on the two principals. This makes for a more somber visual tone, more in tune with the material than the original's satiric discord between the emotional violence of the content and the daytime-TV perkiness of the visual mood. Second, the soundtrack of *Happiness'* opening scene is remarkable for its mix of crisp and clearly articulated dialogue against a consistent hubbub of ambient restaurant noises: general conversation, a waiter's footfalls, the tinkling of cutlery on china. The effect is to heighten the embarrassment of the scene, whose sociality is always audible even as it moves into distinctly intimate territory. In *Life During Wartime*'s equivalent scene, however (just as the background is swallowed up in a soup of gloom), much less of this ambient sound is audible—just the occasional sibilance and murmur of a completely indistinct set of voices, all subsumed in a sullen low-Hertz rumble and hum. The effect of this low murmur of sound is to further abstract the dialogue from a properly public reality and thrust it into a more hypothetical zone set apart from the world. As if in sympathy with this effect, the actors speak their lines in very hushed tones, almost a whisper, adrift in a silence that makes their dialogue more confessional. Third, the repeat scene is shorter by about a minute than the scene that it is mimicking, an acceleration that tends to diminish the intensity and horror of its prototype. Fourth, of course, the dramatis personae have changed. Andy Kornbluth will stage his reappearance in this film, to be sure, but in a later scene; his death ten years before in *Happiness* has removed him from the public field of play, and the tantalizing suggestion at the end of that film that Joy will go on to date Allen—the IT guy with a penchant for Russian roulette sex calls—has here matured into an inevitably difficult marriage. So it is that Allen takes Andy's place on the banquette and in the logic of the scene, unwittingly buying the same Gansevoort collectible (on eBay) and regifting it to the same recipient in the same location exactly a decade later. But that substitution has a further consequence in that it draws into the scene a third party who was strictly unnecessary in the earlier film: a waitress who, upon hearing Allen's voice, begins to summon up the memory of when she first heard it.

But now we really must turn to address the issue of casting, which, like the casting of Aviva in *Palindromes*, raises a host of issues that complicate still further the patterns of difference in repetition that have become apparent here. Joy's transubstantiation from the slight but still average-height figure of Jane Adams into the diminutive, aging pixie-girl stature of Shirley Henderson, her long mane of unruly hair tumbling around an atrocious squint-fringe, is loaded with consequences, not least the extraordinary rise in pitch of her voice, from a relatively resonant if breathy timber to an almost ethereal tremolo of girlish warbling. This change in timbral quality affects the way we attend to the character, her passivity in the scene, and the way she seems to be dreaming it rather than living it. For with this new voice, and the appearance that goes with it, Joy is alienated from the qualities of decisiveness and agency associated with her character in *Happiness'* opening scene. If anything, that streak of stubborn willfulness that even her sisters cannot browbeat out of her has fallen away, and her terminally adolescent defiance has deliquesced into a prepubescent mooniness. The writing, as it were, follows the casting, since we cannot imagine Jane Adams remaining this dissociated from her gathering destiny, and Shirley Henderson's relatively laconic lines follow the drift of the performer away from any sense of authority or control. And so it is, too, for the much more dramatic recasting of Michael Kenneth Williams for Philip Seymour Hoffman in the part of Allen, who in turn is substituting structurally for Jon Lovitz in the role of Andy in this scene—a double substitution made all the more confounding by the fact of the black actor's very dark skin, fit and imposing physique, and the alarming scar running down the middle of his face, as against those elder actors' overweight bodies, pasty skin, and bland physiognomies. And though Williams has done very well to modify his natural speaking rhythms and intonations to a more neutral diction than his usual casting requires (as, for instance, the street bandit "Omar" in the TV series *The Wire*), and tightened his voice to a trembling lachrymosity, still this is far from the colorless nasal whining of Hoffman's turn in the role. Indeed, the very pitching of Allen's lines on the unsteady edge of tears militates against any easy recollection of the psychopathic disaffectedness of Hoffman's Allen; Williams's part is moved by his condition, and in the hilarious apologetic monologue to Joy, the casting once more directly affects the content:

Well, so I thought that I should try to be more open. Because I'm really trying, Joy. No more cocaine. No more crack. No more crack cocaine. No more hanging around doing nothing without a job. No more sarcastic remarks or physical attacks aimed at my boss. No more helping old gang members with burglaries and armed robberies. No more getting into fights with strangers, waking up in the gutter. Oh, Joy! It's been like a never-ending struggle. And I keep fighting it. But it's just this one thing I can't stop, and I'm trying with all my—.

His interruption by the waitress leads to the punch line that this "one thing" is the defining character trait of Allen in *Happiness*: his inveterate sex calling of random strangers. And this leads to some general, very interesting questions about character per se that ought to be approached under this rubric of "eternal recurrence."

Roland Barthes defines character in realist fiction as an effect of repeated patterns of semantic nuclei or "semes":

> When identical semes traverse the same proper name several times and appear to settle upon it, a character is created. Thus, the character is a product of combinations: the combination is relatively stable (denoted by the recurrence of the semes) and more or less complex (involving more or less congruent, more or less contradictory figures); this complexity determines the character's "personality," which is just as much a combination as the odor of a dish or the bouquet of a wine.[41]

When Allen is pathetically trying to confess his sole unconquerable weakness to Joy, having overcome so many destructive proclivities that *we never knew he was subject to*, it is of course inevitable that his confession should be taken out of his mouth and dramatized, since this one trait is the "identical seme" that precisely defines his character. What is so striking here is that, for Solondz, it is only ever *one seme* that needs to traverse and retraverse the proper name, even if all the others are radically changed, in order to determine the "personality" in question and distinguish it from others. Let us be clear that Allen is no longer seriously overweight, an ensconced IT support worker, living alone, disaffected, incorrigibly boring, wearing terrible tweed jackets, a heavy drinker, fetishizing his sexy neighbor, negotiating a relationship with a murderer, or white; he *is*, on the other hand surprisingly fit, a recovering cocaine addict, a recovering crack addict, an unemployed worker whose infrequent jobs end in violent flare-ups with his manager, subject to fits of random violence with strangers, an aider and abettor of the crimes of larceny perpetrated by his old gang members, deeply emotional, inherently fascinating, facially scarred, and black. These are, on any normal accounting, completely different characters, and certainly the principles of nineteenth-century novel writing would never have allowed us to conflate them. However, they *are* the very same character, because a Venn diagram of their respective qualities will show that they share two critical components—a name, "Allen," and a defining fixation and drive—that cannot be alienated or dissolved in the overwhelming tide of semic differences. Solondz insists on this singular repetition as the form of an inescapable fate, passed down a potentially endless chain of avatars and actors, and there is no question of "loving" this fate, per Nietzsche's *amor fati*. There is only the horror of recognition. Allen is "he who sexually abuses women anonymously on the telephone," and no other reconfiguration of the complex of personality will alter this essential element of his being, which is both his greatest curse and the sole source of his considerable jouissance. When the black waitress leans over the table and spits into his face, it is a deferred (though insufficient) payback for the extent of his crimes in *Happiness* and an indication in the present that nothing has changed for him—nothing, that is, but *everything else*. And, what we have not yet said, the recognition that stirs in her and provokes her to this spontaneous reaction is a mediated enactment of the audience's own present-tense realization that despite what we think we can see, *this is Allen* from *Happiness*. Until this moment, and despite her thrice muttering his name, we had no means of identifying Joy's husband beyond his immediate characterization. What the spit in the face does is disclose under that characterization a known character we did not know we were looking at—like the underwear Allen himself is always asking about. "I know who you are. Fucking pervert. What are you wearing underneath your motherfucking skull? [Your] voice is the same, motherfucker." Except, of course, it isn't.

Casting in *Life During Wartime*, where every persona who recurs from *Happiness* (and there are eight of them, as well as two from *Welcome to the Dollhouse*) is played by a new actor, is thus a way of raising the issue of exactly what kinds of repetition it takes to make a character "reappear" outside its original setting. And this, of course, is the underlying question of the sequel as such, whose rationale is predicated on a pattern of allowable repetitions that offers just enough variation to distinguish it from a remake without sacrificing the preponderant infantile (and financial) wish for more of the same. In interviews Solondz can be disingenuous about his position with regard to these questions. "Characters beckon," he has said, explaining in various places that he had a lingering interest in revisiting those characters in altered circumstances.[42] But the facts are much more complicated, given that the extraordinary $5 million budget for *Life During Wartime* (after *Palindromes*, which made only $700,000) turned on the richer prospects of a sequel. "Christine Walker and Elizabeth Redleaf, whose production company Werc Werk Works financed *Life During Wartime*, said Mr. Solondz's 'less acid' approach would attract a broader audience than his films usually do. 'We saw the script as more commercial,' Ms. Walker explained. 'We thought there might be people who didn't see *Happiness* because of its controversial nature, but who've heard Todd's name and are curious about his work.'"[43] Characters "beckon," then, because larger budgets are contingent on the commercial prospects of cashing in on a viable property—the impeccable critical cachet of *Happiness*, which, ten years later, will have mellowed out the immediate storm of controversy over its supposed morals. In order to acquire a cast including Allison Janney, Paul Reubens, Ciarán Hinds, Ally Sheedy, Shirley Henderson, Michael Kenneth Williams, and Charlotte Rampling, you need to offer some assurance to the investors that the run of disasters on your last two pictures will not be repeated, and the best way to do that is to mortgage the most bankable asset you own (the reputation of your masterpiece). *Life During Wartime* is a film made, as it were, on the promise of recycling a certain kind of value, a value associated with a list of character names and relations, a promise that was meant to be broken.

Solondz has been determined to dissociate this film from the mindless repetition implicit in the very concept of a sequel. "It's somewhat misleading to call it a 'sequel,' because it makes people think that the movie is going to have the same kind of character as the earlier film. . . . It's more of a jumping off point than a direct sequel, and more of a quasi-sequel than an actual sequel."[44] Above all, he wants to insist that there has been such a significant modal shift, into the key of *melancholy*, that in truth the line of continuity has been fractured. But we would do well to recall exactly how Freud defined melancholia in relation to a lost love object. The ego, he wrote, refuses to give up on this love and offers it a shelter where it "escapes annihilation," but protected there in its bower of narcissistic absorption, the undead love emanates an unstable radiation of primordial ambivalence and comes to treat the ego itself with much of the sadistic violence that had once been directed (unconsciously) at the love object. Reproaching its bearer, the ego, with the loss of the object, the libido directs blame rather than sympathy at the bereaved subject. Melancholia is the experience of *"identification"* between "the ego and the abandoned object":

> Thus the shadow of the object fell upon the ego, and the latter could henceforth be judged by a special agency, as though it were an object, the forsaken object. In this way an object-loss was transformed into an ego-loss and the conflict between the ego and the loved person trans- formed into a cleavage between the critical activity of the ego and the ego as altered by the identification.[45]

This structure of disavowed abandonment, this internalization and identification of the lost object with the ego itself, has a lot to teach us, not just about melancholia as a state of being but about what must follow all lost "happiness," as its inevitable sequel, when proper mourning does not take place. Let us now make the outrageous assertion that "Todd Solondz," the brand name we (his audience, his critics, his investors) associate with the precious love object *Happiness*, has properly abandoned us and that we have so internalized that lost object that, unbeknownst to ourselves, we have begun identifying with it, berating ourselves for our faithlessness and our inability to sustain the attachment. "Todd" has moved on, and the form taken by his moving on—his other films—are to that very extent *not for us*. In fact, his moving on was immediate and irrevocable. Solondz tells the indicative story of an early screening of *Happiness* at Telluride, when an enthusiastic young fan approached him afterward and told him how "awesome" the film was, especially the child rape scene: "And I knew I was in trouble. And that's why, after that experience, I said 'My movies aren't for everyone, especially people who like them.'"[46]

66 | **Todd Solondz**

Life During Wartime is the homeopathic dose we never knew we needed, to *cure* us of our melancholic condition, wean us off our internalized sadistic attachment to the very film it returns to in order to drain it of its fascination. It is a master class on the truth that *Happiness* is *not for us*, precisely to the extent that we love it. Its lesson in disappointment makes clear the melancholic structure of disappointment itself. So Allen, publicly shamed for his incurable jouissance and consequently abandoned by his wife—indomitable Joy—is driven to repeat the very fate of the man, Andy, who had previously occupied that identical place at the restaurant banquette where ten years before he, too, had presented Joy with the same pewter Gansevoort porringer. It is everything a sequel to *Happiness* should be—repeating the familiar situations, satisfying our curiosity about the characters' fates, reassuring us about their immutable hang-ups—and precisely what it mustn't be: a mockingly imperfect simulacrum of its source and our love object. Peter Bradshaw's review for *The Guardian* can stand in for the contemporary critical reaction: "Interesting and bleakly hilarious as it often is, it will add to an uneasy sense that Solondz is running out of ideas. . . . The director, in his original film, unforgettably offered us the shock of the new. The shock continues to diminish." The byline to the review repeats the dose: "Todd Solondz revisits old ground to diminishing effect." *Diminishment*, then, returns to underscore our conception of the logic of recurrence in Solondz's work. *Life During Wartime* precisely *diminishes* the work on whose shoulders it stands, to mock its melancholic fans with an image of our own melancholia: the film is, to that extent, an abrasive image of *our* not letting go, not Solondz's. Its serial repetitions with variations are homeopathically calibrated to the logic of our inevitable critical dissatisfaction with them, such that we are not even aware that in berating the film for not being *Happiness* we are in fact berating ourselves for having been forsaken by it; the very "cleavage between the critical activity of the ego and the ego as altered by the identification" is what this film obliges us to enact in ourselves.

Solondz himself has always and already moved on, of course, and in truth, *Life During Wartime* is a film that makes all sorts of other, quite different moves in his cinema. But we are detained by its "eternally diminishing returns" because of the nature of its false promise ("pseudosequel") and our own inability to surrender our love for the film it both is and isn't engaged in repeating. Thus, Trish Maplewood (née Jordan) has assumed the role of chief interlocutor with her eldest at-home son, Timmy (now Billy is away at school in Oregon), that Bill once undertook with Billy, and Timmy has assumed Billy's role as the curious maturing child, constantly asking questions of his available parent. The structure is identical to the earlier confabulations between father and son about masturbation and orgasm, and in four excruciating scenes mother and son discuss what it means to "get wet" when a man touches you, the fact that his father is a pedophile rapist, the chances of Timmy himself becoming gay, how anal rape works technically ("where do things go?"), the identity between pedophilia and terrorism, and the importance of "nothing, nothing, ever" getting inside Timmy. (He also gets to say "fuck you, bitch" to his mother, among other jaw-dropping lines.) Functionally, all this is grist to the mill of Solondz's satiric take on the American nuclear family and extends the earlier scenes of intergenerational Maplewood dialogue in intriguing new directions given that the conversation is now across sexual lines (something that will be developed further in *Wiener-Dog*). But, tonally, once again things have altered. Where the scenes between Bill and Billy were touchingly sincere and acted as an ironic refuge from the escalating monstrosity all around them, Trish and Timmy's scenes *are* the monstrosity itself. This is doubtless to be expected from the militant soccer mom who, in *Happiness*, upon hearing that Billy's teacher had a drug problem, explodes into patriotic jingoism of the lowest order: "I'm sorry, but when it comes to drug abuse and children, my children, they should all just be locked up and throw away the key. Billy, I want you to know something, if you ever even *think* of doing drugs and end up dying in a hospital, I'd disown you, that's how strongly I feel about it. I know I may sound harsh, but we're talking about our kids. Not to be too grandiose, but this is the future, the future of our country we're talking about after all." This is the same character who, in this later film, has her eleven-year-old daughter permanently dosed-up on a cocktail of painkillers and antidepressants and who reacts to Timmy's searching ethical questions about terrorism and justice by denouncing all terrorists as evil cowards who "by definition do not have good reasons." Despite the fact that they are shot and edited in much the same way (shot/reverse-shot close-ups and medium two-shots emphasizing intimacy), these scenes in *Life During Wartime* play out in an inverse relation to their counterparts from *Happiness*: moving away from poignancy to its satiric deflation, while Bill and Billy move toward the most astonishing affective intimacy. The disappointment lies in the tonal desecration of what we might have expected to be the film's emotional heart, a quality that therefore has to migrate elsewhere, to some utterly unexpected quarter—namely, Joy's interlocutions with her dead lovers.

Certainly this quality does not migrate to the delayed rendezvous between Billy and his father in Oregon. For here Billy overcomes the dangerous temptation to confess his peculiar familial dysfunction to his dorm friends, only to have its *fons et origo* walk glumly into his room. Dr. Bill Maplewood, as played by Ciarán Hinds, has none of the high-strung nervous energy of the role's previous incumbent, Dylan Baker, whose performance teetered constantly on the verge of hysterical confession, masked by an habitual façade of professionalism. Hinds is stolid, almost monumental, in his role as the recently released convict haunted by what he knows he can no more be rehabilitated of than he would ever want to be. ("Nothing works. It just goes on, forever.") In that sense a kind of dead man walking, a "haint" abroad in the pastel kingdom of Florida, Maplewood has only one last object before him: to reestablish contact with his eldest son in order to make a single determination: whether or not Billy has inherited his father's vice. Their scene is top-heavy with freight it cannot possibly manage in the small space allowed it, temporally and physically. With none of the earlier intimacy available to offset the patent injustices of the unannounced visit itself, their dialogue can only gesture at the conventions of conversation—in the end, it is more like an interrogation, in which Bill takes the active role and Billy is squirming in the hot seat. Over before we know it, the scene has imploded under the weight of its own significance, deliberately failing to live up to our expectations of it (coming as it does after a lengthy quest). Simply, the film wants to frustrate any lingering expectations that it will culminate on an emotional apex the way *Happiness* did on the last scene between these two characters. Once again Solondz has found the means to diminish the structural significance of a sequence whose importance has been determined elsewhere and in advance, by another film, without removing or dismantling it altogether. The encounter is had, the information is imparted—Billy is not gay, does not indulge rape fantasies; this is the right kind of diminished recurrence—but the lighting, the crowded blocking, the setting of the scene all work to dissipate the gravity of this exchange. The stately, dim-lit intensity of their last scene in the Maplewoods' spacious living room in *Happiness* is nowhere to be found in the unforgiving yellow-fluoro glare of the dorm room, the cramped angularity of its space, and the sheer physical awkwardness of Hinds's body within it as he pops gumdrop after gumdrop into his desperately seeking mouth. "Forgive me," he utters mechanically. "There's nothing to forgive," manages Billy. "I mean it's all unforgiveable." It is another lesson in disappointment, which has its roots in the sheer pointlessness of the exercise. That Dr. Maplewood, a qualified clinical psychotherapist with many years of experience, might think that his malady were genetically transmissible, like some kind of Old Testament primogeniture of sin, is as implausible here as that the word "Freud" might be spoken in a scene about inherited sexual proclivities between an ex-con pedophile analyst and a son writing a paper on the sex lives of bonobo monkeys.

Which brings us to Joy's two ghosts—of Andy Kornbluth and of her late husband, Allen—who come to her in what turn out to be the film's most powerful scenes. Here the motif of eternally diminished recurrence is shifted into a psychological register (of guilt and self-recrimination) where its affective power is at a maximum. It is at the end of her somnambulistic episode (discussed earlier), in the deserted generic "Hard Rock" family restaurant, that Joy (Shirley Henderson) encounters the specter of Andy Kornbluth (Paul Reubens), whose sudden appearance as a cadaverous Pee-wee Herman sends a shock of uncomfortable recognition through the audience. Much as Michael Kenneth Williams had helped create a "meta-Allen" in the Venn diagram drawn between him and Philip Seymour Hoffman, so, too, Paul Reubens adds a certain notoriety to Andy—given his infamous arrest for "indecent exposure" (public masturbation) at a Florida porn cinema in 1991. Nothing in the performance style itself, which is more strung-out gothic than campy mischief, suggests the mayhem of the famous "Pee-wee's Playhouse," but to see an actor whose entire career had been identified with a single comic character now channeling the portly Jersey call-center worker is disorientating in a different way again. In effect it is a double diminishment: of Andy now dead and spectral, a mere shadow of himself, and of Reubens, a sad, sunken figment of his former puckish brilliance. And it is that doubly downsized persona who brings to this scene its delicious menace. Since Joy's character is already set at a level of morose passivity that makes drama virtually impossible, and since this revenant is an emissary from her unconscious, it falls to the Other to drive the emotional energy.

Things commence with a held medium shot of Joy alone at the table after the waitress departs; as she slowly opens the menu, a gentle dolly forward brings the camera into a tighter frame-up of her staring vacantly ahead into the void of the empty restaurant as the Larson piano theme strikes up its melancholy chords once more. Into this abyss of reverie, Andy's off-screen "Um" motivates an eye-line match of her attracted look to a slightly low-angle shot of him saying "hi." The film cuts back to Joy's rattled moment of anagnorisis and exclamation of his name and then back and forth between these same shots of Andy asking to sit down and her invitation to do so. So the first shot/reverse-shot alternation in the scene is at this slightly obtuse angle, both shots off eye level and off-center, catching two distinct kinds of isolation. The next phase of the scene, with Joy and Andy seated on opposite sides of the same booth, switches to a far more conventional structure of over-the-shoulder bouncing shot/reverse shots—thirty-four in all, at an average shot length of 3.6 seconds—and covers their reacquaintance and polite reminiscences. The tender side lighting and minimalist sound mix accentuate the intimacy here, the fragile sense of *temps perdu* that even the vestigial imago of Pee-wee Herman can't derail. But a close-up of Joy's sympathetic caress of Andy's hand on the table as he enumerates all the things he misses about life ("I miss . . . I miss my room . . . my laser disc collection") triggers a segue in the scene's third movement. This, the dark heart of the encounter, concerns Andy's shift to a more openly apologetic mode and then into desperation and outright aggression as Joy rebuffs him once more. The shot/reverse-shot structure now toggles between two close-ups of the actors, no longer over-the-shoulder, but center-framed and much more frontal. Thirty-one shots in quick-fire alternation (with an average length of 4.4 seconds) detail their openly weeping faces and the ever deepening chasm between them as the conversation moves to its crisis point:

ANDY: Tell me, Joy, truly, after all that's passed, knowing all you know now, do you wish you could have been with me before?

JOY: [*Pause.*] No.

ANDY: [*Pause.*] Eat shit, you fucking cunt. You think you're improving other people's lives? Saving them, or freeing them, from what? What the fuck do you know about other people? What? Idiot! Why did I kill myself?

The sound mix engineers a reverb effect on the shouted lines, emphasizing the emptiness of the space around them as Andy reverts to his characteristically flamboyant aggression upon rejection. We have been here before, of course, and his recent apology for calling Joy "shit" at the infamous banquette ten years before has suffered its inevitable recantation under the force of Andy's peculiar passion (which we will discuss more fully later in another context). This kind of repetition also marks a decline in the stakes of the game, since there is literally nowhere further for him to go than the suicide that he now regrets. Andy turns the tables on Joy in a final medium shot of them both in the booth, the camera placed at exactly the point where we began the scene four and a half minutes earlier, his body bending hysterically as he points accusingly—"I should have killed you!"—before fading out in a ghostly tremor. Joy's shrinking posture and rapid breathing is the affective residue of a guilt that she can do nothing but rehearse, with eternally diminishing returns, in these moments of existential solitude.

It is thus through the uncanny logic of haunting that Solondz most vividly demonstrates the power of his "diminishing returns" in *Life During Wartime*. Andy makes another appearance later, at Helen's mansion, but the most stunning revenant in this film is that of Allen, whose suicide we discover in a beautiful traveling sequence shot of the conjugal bedroom, motivated by Joy's reconciliatory phone call (after she has exhausted the worthless hospitality of her sisters and mother). There is a brief establishing shot of the ramshackle timber-frame house where they live in some desolate New Jersey working-class district. This is followed by a cut to the shot in question: opening on a tight close-up of the ringing bedside phone and answering machine, then drifting forlornly as Joy leaves her affirmative message on the device—over the rumpled sheets of the bed, past the gently billowing curtains half drawn over the open window, across a wall bearing a framed newspaper story of Joy's good works, down an escritoire with a mounted photograph of the smiling couple—to the floor where Allen's lifeless body lies prone beside a gun and a pool of blood, just as Joy's charged voice speaks the words "I love you." That last touch is at the very far end of the permissible in Solondz's representation of feelings, verging dangerously on sentimentality but saved from it by the austere majesty of the shot that delivers the dose. It is one of those rare moments when an auteurist sensibility is allowed to depart from a strict classicism in order to perforate the ironic prophylactic that otherwise protects us from unwonted exposure to cliché. The suicide itself is a structural repeat of Andy's in *Happiness*, similarly cut to on a phone call with Joy, and which is also narrated in a single traveling shot—of Andy's head in a plastic bag (the one the pewter porringer arrived in) being removed by medics as the detective, momentarily distracted from his call to Joy by a call from his lieutenant, details the cause of death as the camera pulls back to reveal the whole corpse in the suit he wore on his date with Joy. But that shot was deliberately mocking, the sublime strains of Mozart's *Requiem* delivering the pointless suicide over to a nervous laughter. What matters is that the earlier traveling shot is drained of its buoyant comic energy by the saturnine gravity of its repeat in *Life During Wartime*. Sometimes a "diminished return" results in an enhanced mood.

Even this, however, is scarcely a preparation for the return of Allen from this suicidal terminus, at a synagogue washroom during Timmy's bar mitzvah, where Joy has gone to work off the trauma of Andy's third appearance—tonguing her ear for the aliyah. The sequence (as is usual for Solondz's classicism) is told in three parts, each characterized by a distinct cinematographic approach. In the first—a long take—the camera is fixed in position before the large washroom mirror, placed behind a line of vanity sinks and reflecting a row of toilet stalls, where Joy bends to assuage her grief in private. It is from one of these stalls, following an audible flush, that Allen appears, in the mirror's reflection, so our initial image is of Joy's back out of focus in the foreground, her focused face in the mirror looking down despondently into a sink, and Allen's menacing, dark-suited specter at full height in the rear of frame, slightly out of focus. On seeing his image, Joy turns aghast to face his off-screen body, and the focus pulls to her profile looking right, everything else now a murky blur. The lighting is once again somber and golden, glazing the frame in an otherworldly syrup, and the first few lines of dialogue

Figure 9. *Life During Wartime* (2009): Allen's specter

are spoken between Joy's face, right, and the dark shadow of her dead husband in the mirror behind her, flanked on its left side by her own dorsal reflection. It is a bold and arresting composition, very unusual for this director's dialogue scenes but befitting the uncanny register here.

Then, to terminate this long take—a stately 54 seconds long—on her asking whether there is anything she can do, Allen's image walks out of shot, pulling the camera with him, which pans right, leaving Joy behind, crossing a barren stretch of tiles, until it finds him standing at the very right of frame by an electric hand dryer. In the second part of the scene, we settle into a conventional shot/reverse-shot montage of their conversation at close quarters as she stands directly by his side, with each of the setups at close range framed from Joy's height—fifteen close-up shots in total at an average of 5.6 seconds each. The scene's third and final section consists of two shots: first, a two-shot of Allen and Joy from the perspective of the mirror itself—he looking straight ahead into it, she looking in profile up at him as she gently places her hand on his chest—from where she then turns her head to watch him speak in the mirror before them, and, second, a close-up shot of Joy resting her head on Allen's breast and closing her eyes, until he completely fades from view and the harsh sounds of the imminent dance party intrude to forge a bridge to the next scene.

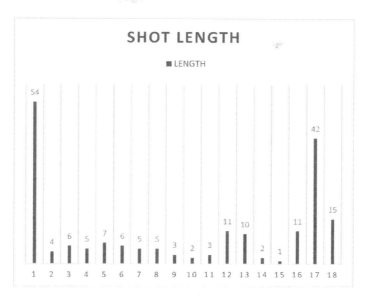

Chart 6. Shot length (in seconds) in "Allen's ghost" scene from *Life During Wartime* (2009)

The graph of the shot rhythm here is dramatic enough to bear a strong comparison with the "first kiss" scene from *Welcome to the Dollhouse*:

The dialogue that this tripartite division of the scene is designed to accommodate runs as follows:

[OPENING SECTION: 1 SHOT]
ALLEN: You're the only one who hasn't forgotten me.
JOY: Allen. Oh.
ALLEN: But you cut and ran.
JOY: Oh, I know. I should never have left you. Never. Please, forgive me.
ALLEN: Too late.
JOY: Oh, but sweetheart, isn't there anything I can do? Anything. Anything to . . . to . . .
ALLEN: Two things.
[MIDDLE SECTION: 15 SHOTS]
JOY: What? What? Tell me.
ALLEN: Delete everything off my computer. All the websites and subscriptions.

JOY: Oh, OK. What else?

ALLEN: Do what I did. Put a bullet through your temple. Gun in mouth is also OK. And then write a note saying, "I am a terrible person. I tried to improve the world but failed. War is evil, but what I did was worse." I will never rest until I see that you know what it is to suffer like I did.

JOY: Oh, Allen, I—I don't know, Allen. I really think I'd prefer taking pills.

ALLEN: Then remember to mix them with alcohol, and to tie a plastic bag around your head afterwards.

JOY: What—What if I end up a vegetable?

ALLEN: You won't.

JOY: But I don't want to die.

ALLEN: You die for me, and I will know you loved me. (Cries.)

[CLOSING SECTION: 2 SHOTS]

JOY: (*leaning into his chest, her hand on his heart*) Allen, did you meet any angels?

ALLEN: Yeah. I mean, sure. Lots of really nice friendly people.

JOY: Do they think this is the right thing to do? An eye for an eye?

ALLEN: Then comes forgiveness.

JOY (*looks up at him, leans in, as he vanishes*)

The precision of this structure, and its limpid statement of the prevailing themes, is striking, particularly so in relation to its various repetitions. This revenant has come to inspire a direct repetition of his own violent suicidal act in its "recipient," Joy, whose preference for pills is itself a repetition of Andy's suicide in *Happiness*, the exact details of which (suicide note, pills, alcohol, and a plastic bag over the head) are restated here in an uncanny recapitulation of the detective's very words in that film—"Suicide note. Looks like a pill-vodka OD, with a bag over his head for a chaser"—and have already been rehearsed in the diner scene with Andy's ghost. Joy has also already apologized profusely to that latter ghost and does so again here, but Allen is every bit the unforgiving specter as his prototype. There is, indeed, no escape from the hall of mirrors in which this scene plays out, literally and figuratively, as the washroom's large mirror dominates the mise-en-scène. Joy's guilt has become a self-consuming mise en abyme, and her two insatiable, parasitic ghosts, between whom she now ricochets, will always have been the Tweedledum and Tweedledee of her unattainable happiness. Joy's

76 | **Todd Solondz**

"hauntology" takes the form of these dead lovers, an endlessly recriminating loop of materials and accusations inherited from another film, recycled and abraded to the point of a single underlying imperative: *kill thyself*, the one thing it had never occurred to her to do in *Happiness*. Above all, what Joy seems unable to do is forgive herself. "Forgiveness" is itself the master theme of *Life During Wartime*, gaining traction through a system of reticulated echoes across the film, and here attains one of its three most powerful statements. The others belong to Billy Maplewood—"It's all unforgivable"—and to Timmy and Mark Wiener, to whom we now turn.

The memorable first exchange between these two most articulate sons of Solondz's main clan systems runs as follows:

> MARK: If it's possible to forgive and forget, or to forgive and not forget, when would you forget but not forgive?
> TIMMY: I think it's possible, if someone does something . . . really terrible to you, like really horrible, something that hurts you so bad, that's so painful, maybe then . . . it's better to forget, and live without all that pain, instead of forgiving and remembering.

When they meet again in the film's final scene, it has become clear that if there is any chance for a resolution of the film's many involuted reiterations of the same motifs, themes, and statements, it lies between these two. Timmy, meanwhile, has done something more or less unforgivable to Harvey, Mark's father, who made the mistake of leaning in for a hug during a loaded conversation about pedophilia with the middle Maplewood child, denouncing him as an "eternally diminished recurrence" of his father's own primary sin, which he sees everywhere after learning of it too late. The accusation is psychologically understandable but morally rotten, as Timmy himself seems to realize, since Harvey is in fact the most "normal" (uncompromised, if uninteresting) character in the Solondz universe—the very reason for Trish's otherwise inexplicable pursuit of him as a partner. When Timmy sees the Wiener father and son packing their goods into a car after walking out of his own bar mitzvah, he comes over to apologize, not to Harvey, but to Mark. On learning that Harvey is moving to Israel, Timmy asks:

TIMMY: But . . . why? Isn't it dangerous there?
MARK: What makes you think there won't be a terrorist attack here? I mean, if I were Al-Qaeda, this part of Florida is a gold mine. Anyway, I don't think he's too focused on survival these days.

The brief conversation thus raises everything the circumvolved family melodrama—mired in self-conscious "sequelitis"—has gone to such elaborate lengths to forestall and disavow but that has nevertheless been running consistently alongside that torrid melancholia—namely, a long series of contextual indicators that *Life During Wartime* has wanted all along to be about, not the Maplewoods and Jordans and Wieners, but the complex subject of its own title. It is critical to note that Solondz's original working title for the film was indeed "Life During Wartime" and that he changed it during production to "Forgiveness" (to mask the disappointment of his plans should the finances run dry and the production get shelved) before reverting to its proper and true title upon release. This is of the greatest importance because it allegorizes the underlying struggle in the film itself: between a family melodrama centered on the theme of forgiveness and sin and a political film addressing the state of the nation during the wars against Afghanistan and Iraq (masquerading as a "war on terror"), and thus between a production conceived as a "sequel" for the producers and a production understood by its own maker as something more pointed and contemporary.

Harvey Wiener has all along been a figure, for Trish, of Israel itself: a not terribly attractive homeland where she can reimagine her faith and family under the sign of a superegoic ethnic duty. Solondz has often joked that the Jordans should be understood as a Jewish family and that Trish's great mistake was to have married a gentile in the first place. "See what happens?" But all of this becomes much more powerfully allegorical after the September 11 bombings and the US state's militarist response, which plunged the Middle East into escalating rounds of political unrest and ethnic bloodshed, not to mention hundreds of thousands of military casualties. And not to mention the militarization of everyday life at home. For in this context, "Israel" becomes a signifier of patriotic American chauvinism itself, pitched against a Muslim Other it cannot think of but as an *uncontainable*, *unintegrable*, and *ungovernable* wolf in the fold.[47] To stand with Israel is to stand bravely against the "evil cowards" who, as Timmy painfully explains to his mother and Harvey, might very well "have a good reason" for doing what they do. "What if your family were tortured, wouldn't you want to do something about it? To protect others?" But this exemplary moral relativism is precisely the style of thinking that "life during wartime" shuts down and dele- gitimizes, indeed criminalizes in the imperial state, by way of a unitary logic of exclusion, just as the film, *Life During Wartime*, has shut down this other, potent dimension of its semantics through a tyrannous (and ironic) application of the hegemonic logic of the sequel and the family knot.

Israel itself, however, has become newly "dangerous" on the basis of these wars in the region (itself clearly indicated through the Jordan pat- ronym) that destabilize the always precarious balance of powers in that apartheid state, whose constituencies articulate with the Arab nations in the region and the sole remaining superstate according to overdeter- mined structures of representation and solidarity. Harvey's departure there can thus be construed as a properly suicidal wish, as his son duly does, given that "survival" is no longer uppermost in his mind after a twelve-year-old boy has wrongly accused him of sexual abuse. Israel is, as he tells Trish on their first dinner date, "where I want to be buried" and thus the locus of a profound death wish throughout the film: "Oh my God," mews Trish, wearing the Hebraic letter ח (Ḥet) around her neck. "Me too! Me too." It is an association ratified upon Joy's visit to Helen, the family apostate, who features a large work of photographic "action art" on her wall and a new tattoo on the inside of her arm.

Helen Jordan is an apostate in more senses than one. The iconic im- age of the Palestinian youth raising an arm like David against the Israeli Defense Force's goliath armored vehicle is so on the basis of a law of association with innumerable other such images and the still more iconic video footage of Tiananmen Square in the late 1980s: eternal recurrence at the level of the image. But the affiliation is crystal clear: both the nar- rativity of the picture and its coloration clearly conduct identification toward the rebel and away from the monstrous military power of the state of Israel (here overtly identified through a Star of David). Helen's antipathy to the Israeli state is then taken an extreme further step by the elaborate flourishes of calligraphy inked onto her skin. As Ally Sheedy explains in an interview, "She also has this tattoo on her arm, which was

Figure 10. *Life During Wartime* (2009): Jihad

really important for him [Solondz] to have, and it says 'Jihad' in Arabic. You can't really read it in the scene—it was cool for me!—but he wanted to have that on her arm, for a lot of different reasons."[48] One of those reasons is to show how geopolitical warfare runs like fracture lines through everyday life and the family, militarizing the spaces of privacy with signs and gestures of violent conflict centered elsewhere. Another is, of course, to satirize the "politics of the image" as such, since nothing is easier, at one level, than to declare your political allegiances with expensive imagery and body art when privilege and distance protect you from the violent consequences others must bear directly. A third is to construct an allegorical triangle whereby Trish is Israel and conservative American values, and Helen is Palestine, the anti-imperial pose of the bohemian artist and what the Anti-Defamation League calls a "Jew-hating Jew," leaving Joy to represent liberal non-commitment and the ambivalence of a "beautiful soul." In any event, that the tectonics of the fracturing Jordan clan are overwritten with the insignia and ideations of a country and a whole region at war (again, the clan is so named for a reason) is by this point painfully clear, in a series of associations that show how "Forgiveness" and "Life During Wartime" are the recto and verso of a single page, a single conception, in this work—one visible through the transparent intensities of the other.

And so we return to Mark Wiener, surely this film's most unexpected diminished recurrence. It is the character's third appearance since he first brought Steve Rodgers to the Wiener home in *Welcome to the Dollhouse*, and he bears a name by which, in certain contexts, Solondz himself has elected to be identified. (Mark's eyeglasses and tech-geek sartorial style bear more than a passing resemblance to the auteur.) We have already considered his appearance in *Palindromes*, where he undertook something of an oracular function, meeting and conversing with Aviva on two occasions and delivering the obsequy at Dawn's funeral. But of all the continuities fleshed out in *Life During Wartime*, Mark's character "arc," if we can call it that, is the most bitterly realistic. He is first anticipated by his father in the second scene, where Harvey is explaining his move to Florida: "My son Mark. He's a great kid. You know, he's a little troubled, just feels a little paranoid, but he's—he's really a very sweet kid. I know. Good heart. Anyway, so he moved down here [to Florida]. I wanted to be near him, you know, help him adjust, make sure that he doesn't get . . . misinterpreted. So I moved here also." Immediately, then, the issue is one of Mark's specialness, his exceptional status as a moral being ("Good heart"), but also his likelihood of being misunderstood and, we surmise, misused. As indeed was the case in *Palindromes*, where his care for Aviva was offset by the general "misinterpretation" of his behavior toward his niece as pedophilia. Mark remains somebody in need of care, then, and specifically paternal care. When Trish asks him, on their first meeting, what he does for a living, his answer confirms his father's solicitous concerns: "Systems analysis. It is [interesting] to me, moderately. Like intermediate-level Sudoku. But I have no illusions that what I do is of interest to anyone else. Even among specialists. I'm something of a functionary. But without ambition or even hope of ambition. I plateaued in grad school then lost interest, except in maintaining a base salary adequate to financing a low-overhead subsistence." It is a classic Solondz speech, delivered with deadpan monotony and a lack of all expression, clear as a computerized readout. So it raises the question of Mark's "trouble," which has been consistent from Solondz's first film to this one: is he autistic or on the spectrum? And if so, how should we conceive of him as a "really sweet kid," as we have some reason to do, despite the obvious inaptitude of the description? We remember him in *Welcome to the Dollhouse* not offering an iota of support to his bullied sister and vanquishing his first spasms of sexuality in order to pursue the good grades that would lead him to grad school. And we recall Joyce Victor in *Palindromes* musing, "That Mark was always a little weird," while her husband retorted, "Seemed pretty regular to me." But we also remember Mark playing Dawn's recording of a piano performance at her funeral and picking up Aviva at the side of the road out of sympathy and showing up to her party because "not coming would be an admission of guilt. You have to hold on to some shred of dignity." Indeed, our recollections of Mark are all complex and variegated, unlike our memories of most other Solondz characters. And this exceptional Fosterian "roundness" is elaborated in order to develop a character so bereft of charisma and charm as to defy memory altogether—the kind of person who never appears in standard Hollywood productions except for ridicule.

Solondz's interest in bringing this character back to life in *Life During Wartime* is, of course, overdetermined by the logic of "sequelizing" already at work in this film, now extended to two other films concerned with the Wieners (*Welcome to the Dollhouse* and *Palindromes*) and thus fostering an active link between the two families. But this return comes, once again, with a considerable difference in the charge of the character in this new context, beginning with the casting. For Mark Wiener had always taken the distinctive shape and form of Matthew Faber, an actor whose distinctively large head, thinning hair, overbite, long neck, defensive scowl, and gangly body had always suggested a superannuated teenage nerd lost in the world he was trying so hard to master. So it comes as something as a shock to discover Mark Wiener in the body of the rounder and more substantial Rich Pecci, whose physical quotient of "nerdiness" is now confined to the thick, dark-framed spectacles that dominate his face and who therefore has to manifest a certain asocial, autistic quality in his monotonous speaking voice and unsmiling stare. What had been a character grounded in a specific body type and tone of voice is thus reduced to something of a caricature and consequently drained of much in the way of audience interest. He is imported into this scenario principally as a counterpoint to young Timmy, who is drawn to him, much as Aviva was, as a source—not of sympathy—but of involuntary honesty in a world of routinely deceptive appearances. Nobody is likely to misinterpret Mark's character as we find it here, after all; it

82 | **Todd Solondz**

has become a type. And the only reason we have to insist on the identity between what we find here and the Mark Wiener of two other films is, once again, a singular obsession or drive.

That drive has to do with a mental abolition of the present in the name of a future event from whose imagined perspective "nothing else matters." In *Welcome to the Dollhouse*, that future state is, of course, college. Mark's coup in securing the services of Steve Rodgers as lead singer in his high school band, the Quadratics, is reduced to a single advantage: "The point is, is this is exactly what I needed for my college résumé. With this kind of substantial extracurricular activity, I'm going to have it made!" When Dawn asks whether he ever thinks about girls, Mark fires back, "What, are you kidding? I want to get into a good school! My future's, like, important?" He even has the last line of the film: "Don't be stupid," he says of Dawn's preference for not going to Disneyworld with the Hummingbirds choir. "If nothing else it'll look good on your college résumé." There are residues of this particular species of chiliasm in *Palindromes*, as when Aviva asks him whether Dawn ever found any happiness: "Yeah, there were moments. Moments . . . here and there. Maybe when she got into Rutgers, I guess, I don't know." But for the most part, Mark's apocalyptic imagination has taken a distinctly ontological turn. His speech on determinism and fate is grounded in a vision of inevitable environmental degradation, extinction, and the heat death of the universe: "Genes and randomness: that's all there is, and none of it matters. . . . Really, it makes no difference, since the planet's fast running out of natural resources and we won't survive to the next century." When we meet again in *Life During Wartime*, however, this planetary millenarianism has mutated into a historical, geopolitical, and economic reassessment of the rapidly altering balance of powers. Asked by a flummoxed Trish if he is "seeing someone," Mark's response is immediate: "No, I'm more focused on China. Everything else is history." And again at the end of the film, in his colloquy with Timmy, after the younger Maplewood boy has broken down while recounting the story of his father, Mark can issue no sympathy, since, as he says, "It's like freedom and democracy. In the end, China will take over, and none of this will matter." The unpopular kid, the nerd who suffers high school only for college, evolves into the ontological pessimist and thence into the geopolitical realist. The sole constant is the insistence that "nothing matters" but the singular event—Ivy League admission, planetary extinction, China's irresistible hegemony—that allows the ego to annihilate the Real, which keeps it in such a stunted state of loveless solitude. This inevitable recurrence of the Mark Wiener syndrome in *Life During Wartime* nevertheless has the singular advantage of "red-shifting" the film's preoccupation with US foreign policy and the Middle East much farther east, allowing "China" to serve as a larger frame in which all of these other conflicts and passions will finally "not matter" and so "be history." If, as somebody once said, it's easier to imagine the end of the world than the end of capitalism, Mark is here to remind us that in many senses it is easier to imagine China's ascendancy than the end of the world: not so much an end of capitalism as its sublation in the planetary extension of a single-party superstate, part capitalist, part communist, and entirely un-American.

What are we to make, finally, of these insistent repetitions, none quite as satisfying as the last, running through the Solondz oeuvre like the twists and turns of a fun-fair mirror maze? In one sense, of course, it is of the essence of all comedy. "It is certainly trying to a man's dignity," as George Eliot once wrote, "to reappear when he is not expected to do so: a first farewell has pathos in it, but to come back for a second lends an opening to comedy."[49] It is an insight mirrored in Karl Marx's contemporary attribution: "Hegel remarks somewhere that all great world-historical facts and personages occur, as it were, twice. He has forgotten to add: the first time as tragedy, the second as farce."[50] Henri Bergson analyzes the key function of repetition in laughter according to its tendency to disclose "the deflection of life towards the mechanical" in the midst of daily experience. "And laughter will be more pronounced still, if we find on the stage not merely two characters [the same], but several, nay, as great a number as possible, the image of one another, who come and go, dance and gesticulate together."[51] But of course repetition is also an essential feature of tragedy, for tragedy cannot work without the fateful repetitions of character on the horizon of destiny. For Gilles Deleuze, repetition is to be thought of as the primordial element in which the tragic and the comic lay curled in potential, to be separated out by formal development:

> Comic repetition works by means of some defect, in the mode of the past properly so called. The hero necessarily confronts this repetition so long as "the act is too big for him": Polonius's murder by mistake is comic, as is Oedipus's enquiry. The moment of metamorphosis, tragic repetition,

84 | **Todd Solondz**

follows. It is true that these two moments are not independent, existing as they do only for the third moment beyond the comic and the tragic: the production of something new entails a dramatic repetition which excludes even the hero. However, once the first two elements acquire an abstract independence or become genres, then the comic succeeds the tragic as though the failure of metamorphosis, raised to the absolute, presupposed an earlier metamorphosis already completed.[52]

We can begin to get a true sense of the stakes of Solondzian repetition if we insist that, in it, no "metamorphosis" ever comes. It is as if blocked by some malfunction in the nature of the comic repetition itself, which is here not defined by an act "too big" for the protagonist. That is to say, the defect for Solondz lies not in the actor or person but in the past itself. In what he persists in calling his "sad comedies," what is repeated is the absence of any conditions for a tragic, or a comic, act in the first place. Neither can we properly refer in this context to Deleuze's notion of the "three repetitions," used to underscore the significance of Nietzsche's "eternal return." "The highest test is to understand the eternal return as a selective thought, and repetition in the eternal return as selective being," he writes.

> The selection occurs between two repetitions: those who repeat negatively [comic heroes] and those who repeat identically [tragic ones] will be eliminated. They repeat only once. The eternal return is only for the third time: the time of the drama, after the comic and after the tragic. . . . The eternal return is only for the third repetition, only in the third repetition. The circle is at the end of the line. . . . The Negative does not return. The Identical does not return. . . . Only affirmation returns—in other words, the Different, the Dissimilar. . . . Only the excessive returns.[53]

Todd Solondz, however, seems to have been concerned with staking out the grounds of a *fourth* repetition. There would seem to be, over and above the comic hero of the "first" repetition and the "tragic" hero of the second, as well as the Nietzschean hero of *amor fati* in the third repetition, a character type of the *fourth repetition*, which I am tempted to call the *loser*, who lives out his repetitive fate in an arc of diminishment described by the drive. It is precisely the drive as such—the compulsion to negate the present, to make anonymous sex calls, to rape children, to collect children's toys, to become a teenage mother—that defines the Solondz protagonist. But this is also what deprives him or her of the full potential for tragic destiny (in recognition or anagnorisis). In the final analysis, the drive is what prevents metamorphosis and forestalls the dynamics of action in a cycle of diminishing returns that is not exactly comic either. It is, rather, "pathetic" in a fully postmodern sense (and not at all the sense of Aristotle's *pathos*). The affect of the Solondz loser is a suffocating feeling of the *pathetic* that disallows any catharsis or proper identification but the kernel of which is a true immortality, since it consistently resurrects the carapace of a committed subject around its serial mortifications. "It just goes on, forever," as Dr. Maplewood tells Billy. This is the logic of the fourth repetition, the repetition of eternally diminished returns.

It is notable that Solondz does allow certain characters to seize the opportunity of a true act, but these are by definition never the protagonist. Rather, they appear in the list of "minor" or secondary characters, as if to remind us what such an act might look like and how distant we are from one in the narrative foreground. In *Welcome to the Dollhouse* the acts belong to Brandon, who both kisses Dawn Wiener and then "lights out for the territory" on his father's threat to send him to a military academy. In *Happiness* it belongs to Kristina, who murders Pedro the doorman after he rapes her in her apartment. In *Palindromes* it belongs to Earl (Joe/Bob), who kills himself after his accidental homicide of a young girl. In *Life During Wartime* it belongs to Allen, whose suicide is existentially authentic in the profoundest sense (unlike Andy's). And there is only one true act in either *Dark Horse* or *Wiener-Dog*, which we are about to consider, and which belongs, again, to Brandon. The protagonists, on the contrary, are withheld from the dimension of the act by their drives. "Insofar as the aim of the drive is not to reach its goal but to enjoy, we enjoy our endless circulation, our repetitive loop," writes Jodi Dean.[54] But "enjoyment" here does not mean what it does in everyday parlance; rather, it specifies an intensity of affective immanence that entails as much suffering (moral, legal, interpersonal, etc.) as it does pleasure. "I fucked them," a devastated and overwrought Bill Maplewood tells a teary Billy about the fate of his school friends. "What was it like?," Billy asks. "It was . . . great," his father replies as they both break down in wracking sobs. "Enjoyment" carries within it this terrible

86 | **Todd Solondz**

quotient of horror and misery, and it is in the endless circuits around this core of affective excess that Solondz's protagonists are helplessly trapped. Their repetitions and recurrences are cyclical in the worst sense, each circuit around the radioactive kernel of their desire exposing them to just that much more radiation poisoning. None of them can muster the courage or willpower to cut the Gordian knot of their involuted fate, which is in them more than them, for them there is no decisive act, just a permanent detour through the "deadly space between."

All of which leaves us begging the question of Dawn Wiener herself, who is neither trapped in an endless circle of jouissance nor able to commit herself to an act. And it is therefore perfectly apposite that Solondz has been most inconsistent about her reappearances, the very nature of her repetitions. After we last see her trapped at the back of the school bus on the way to Disney World with the Hummingbirds in *Welcome to the Dollhouse*, the logic of narrative and semantic organization in the film has implied that things look grim for Dawn: her only true friend (her former bully, Brandon) has departed for parts unknown; her plan to rid herself of the terrible blight of her perfect sister, Missy, has backfired, and Missy is more than ever the family favorite; Dawn has subjugated herself to the will of the institution and the family in acquiescing to the Disney trip; her clubhouse has been dismantled; her object of desire, Steve, has proven his unworthiness; and her father (a silent partner beside her truly awful mother) has suffered a total nervous breakdown. Any idea that things might get better once she graduates to senior high has been rudely disappointed in advance by her unsympathetic brother, Mark. So it comes as little surprise when, some years later, *Palindromes* opens with her funeral service, with suicide the stated cause of death. Of course, this posthumous return is rather shocking, even for Solondz, since the nature and specificity of her act has been denied us, which is why it cannot qualify, the way that Earl's and Allen's suicides do, as an act in the first place. It comes across instead as an abrupt authorial fiat, and Dawn is felt henceforth in this film merely as a field of gravitational pressure affecting Aviva's quest. The question is whether or not Aviva is sufficiently like Dawn to emulate her suicidal passage or different enough to pursue her own course. The end of the film is a potent nod in the latter direction, since Aviva has what Dawn manifestly never did: a drive, an overriding need to exist and compulsion to enjoy.

Our lingering dissatisfaction with this fate of one of Solondz's most appealing characters—the sense that she has been cavalierly sacrificed to a more or less cynical device in a film that, as it were, grows on her grave—is then given the most astonishing reversal in *Wiener-Dog*. The very name of this film has already, so to speak, resurrected her, since it is identical to the nickname Dawn bore through the bleak years of Benjamin Franklin Junior High School, and we have been sensitized to her hovering presence through the first episode of the film, which literalizes all too bathetically the eponymous title in an actual dachshund dog, christened "Wiener-Dog" by Remi the cancer survivor. This is a unique variation of the logic of eternally diminished recurrence, this sudden stab of disappointment that, not Dawn (as we might have hoped), but an actual wiener dog will supply the thread of this film—another cruel twist in the tail of Solondz's ongoing "meanness" toward the middle Wiener child. But all of this is an elaborate feint, softening us up for the extraordinary transformation undertaken by the film's second episode, altogether this auteur's most moving and affirmative passage in over twenty years of filmmaking. For here, in the luminous form of Greta Gerwig's graceful beauty—which cannot be dimmed by her still appalling wardrobe—is Dawn Wiener herself, working in a suburban veterinary surgery, living alone in a dismal low-rise apartment complex, heroically rescuing the other eponymous figure (whom she will rechristen "Doody") from her nasty fate under gas and scalpel. All at once, as her identity becomes clear during a conversation in a Food Mart, we realize not that Dawn's suicide and funeral did not take place but that they have been miraculously *undone* by a new moral logic, in the decisive, solitary exception to Solondz's law of diminishing returns. Wiener-Dog may have died, but she also never died and is now "sublated" into a single image of care and love with the other wiener dog of the film.

Surely the key to the mystery of Dawn's miraculous reappearance is inherent in this image, since it so clearly instantiates a principle of immortality that goes by no other name than love. Dawn's overriding need is the universal subjective requirement of a reciprocal embrace in which the self-evident limitations of being one, being singular, is dissolved in the fluid radiance of a two. Dawn is the living embodiment of what we are about to designate as a certain *excremental quality* of individuation: she incarnates the *pure shit* of being one, alone, and she

Figure 11. *Wiener-Dog* (2016): the wiener-dogs

knows it. The nuclear family provides her with nothing but confirmations of this excremental value, as do the institutions and organizations that constrain her to her place. It is only in fantasy that the truth speaks its illimitable name. A series of to-camera addresses during a dream sequence in *Welcome to the Dollhouse* articulates the term: "I love you so much," says Mrs. Wiener; "I love *you*, Dawn," her father urges from his sickbed; "Me too, I love you," chimes Mark; "Oh, Dawn!," swoons Brandon, "I love you!"; and Steve Rodgers croons an impassioned "I love *you*!" before the whole population of her junior high school agrees in a rousing chorus: "Oh, Dawn, we *love* you!"

> "I love you." That small sentence is usually thought to be completely meaningless and banal. Moreover, people sometimes prefer to use other, more poetic, less commonplace words to say "I love you." But what they are always saying is: I shall extract something else from what was mere chance. I'm going to extract something that will endure, something that will persist, a commitment, a fidelity. . . . The locking in of chance is an anticipation of eternity. And to an extent, every love states that it is eternal: it is assumed within the declaration.[55]

Nobody has yet uttered "I love you" to Dawn Wiener, who is not (despite the weight of an entire culture against her) unlovable, as even

The Law of Diminishing Returns | 89

her sworn enemy, Brandon, was obliged to approve. It is her very all-consuming need to hear the words, to feel the embrace, that has brought her back from the dead; the eternity implicit in them, in its unspoken potentiality, overrides the death drive. And it is critical to state that this need to be loved is *not* a drive in that Freudo-Lacanian sense. It is more in the vicinity of a right, or an entitlement, that each of us, in our very excremental worthlessness, may miraculously come to expect at least once in our lives.

For all that, there is nowhere in particular for Dawn to go in this space of miraculous reappearance, since she is trapped by the entropy of circumstance in a round of low wages, joblessness (she cannot now return to the vet whence she stole the dog), hunger, and despair. Resurrection is not enough, then, however moving it may be, in a film that still accepts the brutal determinism of American fate. What is required is the touch of a true act that can break Dawn out of the shallow routine of the isolated working poor, an act that nothing in the Solondz universe has prepared us to believe in—an act, that is to say, of love that answers precisely Dawn's unfulfilled expectation.

We can put it this way: Dawn's return is, this one exceptional time, *not* a diminished return, but it nevertheless lacks dynamic force. It shimmers as a vibrant potentiality. It remains, then, to Brandon to supply the missing affirmation, as it had in *Welcome to the Dollhouse* almost twenty years before. His kiss, masked behind the spurious threat of rape, had been that film's most decent and transformative act, taking an unexpected latency (the desire implicated within a bully's animosity) and forcing an explicit, transfiguring avowal (which Dawn, her imagination caught by the spurious "love object" Steve, had not been able to reciprocate). From the moment that he calls out to her "Wiener-Dog!" in the Food Mart, this older Brandon (Kieran Culkin) carries with him a moral ambivalence that turns on a dime until the final seconds of the episode: will he recur to his original belligerence and cruelty, or will he persevere in the glow of his prior fidelity to Dawn's worth? The blankness of Culkin's performance, the sheer emptiness of his gaze for much of the sequence (not a quality we associate with the actor Brendan Sexton III, who continues to play markedly psychopathic characters to this day), makes him uniquely difficult to parse, an indeterminacy amplified by the character's use of opiates throughout. Dawn's mute place by his side in the van that takes them to his brother's house in Ohio is punctuated by querying side glances and hopeful smiles, but there is nothing to indicate the deeper significance of his invitation to her to accompany him. It is a special kind of suspense, contoured by what we have come to expect from Solondz's filmed "relationships" (constantly thwarted as they are by closeted pedophilia, lovelessness, homicide, secret infidelities, disease, cynicism, and the impersonal will to breed). Expectation tilts in favor of affirmation the moment we realize the purpose of Brandon's trip West—to inform his Down syndrome–affected brother of their father's recent death from alcohol abuse. The moving scene where he finally convinces Tommy that their father has passed away ends in a tearful embrace and the promise that he, Brandon, will quit heroin rather than rob Tommy of his last remaining blood relative. Suddenly the reasons behind what Dawn calls Brandon's "elusiveness, intractability" become clear, and the way is smoothed for some still greater affirmation to come. But our psychic defenses have never been more prepared for disappointment; there has been altogether too much affirmation as it is, and when Dawn happily gives Doody to Tommy and April, it is truly as if we have reached the outer limits of Solondz's hitherto closeted humanism. Surely the only plausible outcome as Brandon drives them away is his summary rejection of Dawn and the foreclosure of the miraculous loop opened by her resurrection. Everything in Solondz's cinema to this point has prepared us to accept this bitter pill, which never comes. For in the filmmaker's most unexpectedly romantic turn, Brandon answers Dawn's pathetic, self-defeating questions about their future with a silent gesture of limitless avowal—his hand descends upon hers and grips it tenderly. The kind of thing that runs like an insufferable cliché through Hollywood and independent American film alike, the symbolic economy of the heteronormative love story, here injects itself like a foreign agent into a cinematic universe predicated on its absence. And the effect is astonishing, the hackneyed *gestus* cleansed of its stereotypy by the sheer unlikelihood of its appearance here.

Dawn's return has been vouchsafed to oversee this remarkable double negation: not only does the episode singularly contradict the law of diminishing returns, but in so doing, it triggers the audience's disbelieving recognition of something altogether alien to the world it punctures from within: a simple "yes." "Yes" looks very different when it is sprung from

Figure 12. *Wiener-Dog* (2016): the miraculous affirmation

negation, and here, it is worth saying, the negation is not strictly local. There is little in the episode itself to protect it from cynical accusations of sentimentality and authorial capitulation to market expectations. Rather, the episode works because of its uniquely exceptional status with regard to the rest of the film and the entire Solondz oeuvre around it; specifically, it works in relation to the dreadful fate meted out to Dawn Wiener in previous films. In a cinematic universe governed by the diminished returns of empty circulations around the nidus of jouissance, and the affective malaise of the loser, a single act offered in contradiction shines with irresistible effulgence, whereas that same act inserted into a universe of liberal humanistic values smacks offensively of manipulative emotional blackmail. I will not go so far as to say that the otherwise unbroken law of eternally diminishing returns has been set in place precisely to allow this one radiant moment of comeuppance. It can more modestly be suggested that just such a moment is a possible consequence of the career-long, twenty-year restraint that it shatters in an instant. It has, as they say, been earned, and we have earned the right to enjoy it.

Screens of Fantasy, Durations of the Real

The scene that reestablishes the heightened ironic tone of the Solondz voice, immediately after this retreat from it, lies at the very opposite end of this cinema's spectrum of effects—the interpolated "Intermission" song and tongue-in-cheek travelogue sketch of the Odyssean wanderings of Wiener-Dog, the dachshund. This bizarre and amusing episode, separable from the rest of film and without any narrative consequence, effectively apotheosizes and terminates the "feel-good" part of the movie; after it, we move into the Danny DeVito and Ellen Burstyn chapters, which are among the darkest in the Solondz canon. Set to a jaunty country-western-style ballad about Wiener-Dog's epic journey across the primordial American landscape, the intermission is both poignantly "meta-cinematic" (in that it internalizes a long-lost cinematic experience to a work that will only be seen at home on digital video) and purely phantasmatic. It is to this latter aspect of his work that we must now turn, the aspect that, in various ways, departs most strongly from Solondz's presiding classicism and the aesthetic realism it tends to promote. The *Wiener-Dog* intermission is, to be sure, a satire of an intermission and takes advantage of the chapterized structure of this film to drive a sequestered formal wedge deeply into the content of the work; to that extent, its effect is to restore the classicism of its delivery, hard on the heels of the artist's most romantic moment. And yet, though the tone is one of an almost purified irony, there is a further dimension to this episode that recommends our careful attention to its aesthetic purpose. There is something else at work here beside irony—namely, an insight into the film's ample quotient of fantasy and dream work, which it now raises to the level of a dominant. The dachshund's voyage is a projection onto the film's surface of its underlying utopian yearnings: a purposeful forward march, in a major key, across all the landmarks of the nation—against which the actual contents of the individual episodes (cancer treatment, entrapment, poverty, drug addiction, death in the family, alienation from work, isolation, old age, and misanthropy) weigh as so many distasteful reminders of the American "reality principle." The *pleasure principle*, then, and its dilation in the realm of fantasy, is what the intermission so delightfully enshrines, and in doing so, it reminds us of how ample this seam of materials is in Solondz's cinema.

It is in *Welcome to the Dollhouse* that the dimension of fantasy is first broached, and although that film includes an intermittent amount of subjective reverie on the part of the protagonist throughout, it is in one scene in particular that the realist surface is thoroughly perforated:

The Law of Diminishing Returns | 93

the one we have just recounted above, the dream sequence near the very end of the film, set during Dawn's night on the New York streets in search of her missing sister. The wish fulfillment of the scene (in which everybody tells Dawn that they love her) is perfectly straightforward, and the comedy of its articulation is offset neatly by the inevitable wake-up moment afterward. Fantasy screens the necessarily implausible, impossible supplement to reality: the desperate subjective kernel of desire, thwarted by quotidian life, imposing its desiderata on the disappointing figures of the day—Mother, Father, Brother, and so on.

It is not until *Happiness* that Solondz begins to develop his own distinctive and highly effective phantasmatic space, which has been a mainstay of his cinema ever since. The film's memorable fifth sequence begins in an entirely different key, and tone, from the previous scenes. To an elegant if cloying Robbie Kondor piano and flute theme, we first see joggers, families, and gay couples out and about in a brightly lit park of supersaturated green, in a gentle panning shot that ends on a slightly menacing over-the-shoulder silhouette of the rear of Dr. Bill Maplewood's (Dylan Baker's) head, as he contemplates this hyperreal *déjuner sur l'herbe*. Without a break in the affirmative music, the next shot is a close-up of a semiautomatic rifle, which Bill is locking and loading, preparing for the mayhem that duly follows: a reverse tracking shot finds him blasting picnickers and passersby indiscriminately, with a look of absolute contentment on his face. Brief interpolated shots of contact wounds and general panic are followed by a stable low-angle shot of Bill, walking left, rifle in hand, and then stopping to consider his work. We then cut to an audacious finale—a close-up shot of Bill's awed profile tilts down and cranes up simultaneously, and as we achieve greater elevation, Bill comes to stand in the still center of a lush pasture of the dead and dying, seen directly from above.

This bravura passage is linked to the scene that follows, in the office of Bill's psychiatrist, by a sound bridge: "And how is this different?," asks his shrink about what now appears to be a recurrent dream, to which Bill responds, in a low-angle medium shot, "I don't kill myself at the end." Retrospectively justified as the subjective fantasy of the troubled psychiatrist-pedophile, the episode is designed not to shed any clinical light on his condition but to detonate a disorienting charge of psychosis in the diegesis. Fantasy obtrudes into the real world as a higher-order

94 | **Todd Solondz**

Figure 13. *Happiness* (1998): Dr. Maplewood's fantasy

reality: the Real of Bill's uncontrollable and dangerous desire, which is so much more pleasurable to look at than the dispiriting New Jersey locations of the rest of the film. We experience it, on a first view, as something actually happening; the sound bridge to the clinical session cushions the violent blow but never quite discharges it, since such savagery is now known to be inhabiting the film's most "respectable" figure. By such means does Solondz carve out a critical space within the film, the deeply uncomfortable space of Bill Maplewood's desire, to which we are brought into radical proximity before we even know what it portends and before an entire apparatus of identification devices (point-of-view cinematography, eye-line matches, and the predication of cinematic suspense on the will of the character) fixes our deepest identification with this most diseased of all the film's sick personae.

The closest we come to this interior proximity again in *Happiness* is in a later scene between Joy Jordan (Jane Adams) and Vlad the Russian taxi driver (Jared Harris) in her parents' home, which, while not resorting to direct phantasmatic depiction, nevertheless deploys powerful cinematic techniques to open up for us the desperate immensity of Joy's desire. As Vlad sits to strum and belt out an emotionally charged version of Joe Brooks's "You Light Up My Life," we cut to the first in a set of four luminous close-ups of Joy's wide-eyed face, intercut with powerful close-ups of Vlad's intensely focused visage. The third and fourth close-ups are further animated by a subtle but inexorable leftward dollying around their subjects, imparting true salience and depth to the already pronounced side light of their faces. This is as close as we come in Solondz's cinema to a fully subjectivized set of alternating point-of-view shots in the space of mutual desire. We are inveigled to see the sleazy Russian exactly as Joy sees him: a sensitive, passionate man, full of spontaneous love for his English-language teacher. She herself will never look as beautiful, flushed with arousal, eyes wide and unblinking, lips parting slowly in a yielding invitation. Here, fantasy is filtered directly into the scene of reality, allowed to penetrate it from within with bolts of blinding faith and optimism, which nothing in the rest of film gives us any reason to credit. The pleasure principle trumps the reality principle for a moment by the power of sheer desperation. Of course disappointment will follow—Vlad will turn out to have robbed her and cheated on his partner—but nothing can take away from Joy the one true look of joy she is allowed in two long films as she walks to work as a substitute teacher the next morning through the picket line, oblivious to the jeers of the other teachers she is scabbing.

Solondz's two greatest fantasists—Scooby in *Storytelling* and Abe from *Dark Horse*—provide ample material for the mapping of this kind of territory. "Non-Fiction," indeed, features one of the most lurid fantasy episodes in Solondz's career. As his friend Stanley leans down to perform fellatio on the recumbent Scooby to the strains of Belle and Sebastian, we track in over his pot-smoking profile to a psychedelic poster of rainbow swirls, which, in a seamless process shot, begins swirling in earnest, only to be consumed by a raging fire across the screen, that diminishes to reveal Mr. and Mrs. Livingstone being burned alive at the stake in their front yard as the camera pans left to reveal Scooby watching intently their howls of agony, and a voice behind him calls out "Hey, Scooby!," which he pivots to meet in the person of his idol, Conan O'Brien, who invites his acolyte to be a guest on his show, and they walk to the curb where a TV is tuned to their appearance together later that night, that we zoom into and merge with in a perfect pastiche of Conan O'Brien's *Late Night* talk show. This effortless, dreamy cascade of images and movements coheres into a unified phatasmatic space, where Scooby's simple wish fulfillments reign supreme. Unlike the Dawn Wiener fantasy scene, this one has inherited enough of the violence of Bill Maplewood's dream to underscore a prevailing psychosis, and the entire episode is so giddily playful and imaginative, so flushed with the love of cinematic illusion, that it serves as a new outer limit to the artist's classicism. For with this brief, 110-second sequence, Solondz relaxes all of his strictures, allows his camera to roam and drift, forestalls the temptation to settle into shot/reverse-shot rhythms, and indulges the capacity of the medium to engender teeming worlds unmoored to the reality principle.

Here it is worth exploring an unlikely comparison with the work of another filmmaker who is similarly committed to a ruthlessly logical cause-and-effect universe that, here and there, is punctured by the delirious fantasies of his characters. I am thinking of Luis Buñuel, whose work subsequent to his early collaborations with Salvador Dalí can be seen to traverse two overlapping spaces: the space of a pitiless social reality, where poverty, domination, exploitation, and empty ritual dictate the fixed terms of a divided world, and the space of vivid individual fantasy and dream, where illogic, fevered association, desire, and compression distort and deface the edifice of the Real. It is always important to insist of Buñuel that these two spaces are not simply opposed or merely compensatory in any facile binary sense but describe the recto and verso or, better, the self-inverting surfaces of a Möbius strip, whose looping figure serves to delineate the structural properties of capitalist lived experience. The great Catholic apostate and the atheist Jew converge around the cinematic form of this critical dialectic between alienation and fantasy, logic and il-logic, oppression and inner freedom. For either, it amounts to an aleatory and oneiric augmentation of his films' dominant classicism at the level of enunciation—a tactical negation of that stance in pockets of febrile subjectivity and inwardness. And for both, this is precisely a question of their higher satirical intent, since in either case the projected fantasy does not merely expose the otiose daydreams of a foolish individual but also conveys enough stylistic energy to contradict the social reality that provoked it in the first place. Buñuel's dream sequences, like Solondz's, conduct a charge of truth that never fully evaporates once the narrative starts up again. In them, desire attains to an autonomous agency within the field of forces that defines the film, able at key points to seize control of the cinematic means of production and flood the space with irrepress-ible (and inadmissible) subjective materials.

The Law of Diminishing Returns | 97

Of no character is this truer than of Abe Wertheimer, protagonist of *Dark Horse*. Not only is his narrative arc driven by the absurdity of his fully avowed desires (to woo and win Miranda, to collect all the action figures, to openly defy his father, who both houses and employs him), but the string of fantasy sequences in the film's second half further demonstrates the unyielding subterranean tenacity of his as yet unavowed ones. The first of these, immediately following his bathroom altercation with Mahmoud, concerns a radical transformation in his relationship with the only character who genuinely cares for Abe: his office helpmate and protector, Marie (Donna Murphy), who here morphs from dowdy old maid to prowling cougar, occupying an upscale architect-designed house and driving a Ferrari, strutting with the open sexual purpose of seducing her boss's son. Yet this seduction scene is simultaneously another mentor scene, with the significant difference that now Marie's advice is harsh and cynical: she scorns Abe's empty talk of suicidal thoughts and encourages him to act; she implies that he'll still be living with his parents at fifty and offers her brutal verdict—"you're a cheapskate and a freeloader," "grow up, no one needs you." The genius of this scene is that in "traversing the fantasy," allowing himself to explore his unadmitted desire for the otherwise merely matronly and selfless Marie, Abe discovers the hard kernel of self-knowledge that her imago otherwise obscures. Drawn to what his fantasy proposes as her hunger for him, Abe is nevertheless awkward and defensive as always; he signally fails to reciprocate or break out of his sexually ruinous habits of teetotalism and blowhardism. And so the fantasy gives him back a true image of himself, of which he appears otherwise oblivious.

By far the longest of these sequences, at well over seven minutes, comes directly after what we later understand to have been Abe's terrible accident in his yellow Hummer as he tears out of the company parking lot on learning of his termination. We begin with Abe still driving his vehicle in a fury, his mother (Mia Farrow) alongside him riding shotgun and seeming to offer her usual palliating bromides, a mask that rapidly falls away. Advising him to "face the truth" and dropping the bombshell that she and her husband had "written [Abe] off as a failure years ago," this phantasmatic mother, all smiles and tender charm, has imbued the cynical realism of the dream Marie. Her lessons are particularly bitter, setting up the uneven terms of the rivalry between him and his brother,

98 | **Todd Solondz**

Richard, as an innate, biological given. Richard himself (Justin Bartha) appears in the backseat to underline the efforts he put in to achieve his various academic and professional successes as against the obvious laziness and failure of his brother. Ganging up on the increasingly irate Abe for his "attitude problem," this pair of familial specters lances every boil on his diseased ego with laser precision. "Fuck both of you!," he explodes, eventually pulling over and trying to yank them forcibly from the Hummer while they lock themselves in and Abe out on the street. This is all shot in uncomfortable close-ups, Richard leaning in over the shoulder, Mrs. Wertheimer craning toward us in the driver seat, Abe himself expostulating bitterly in profile but bathed in radiant sunshine, as if to underscore the emotional and psychological veracity of the pitiless takedown. Enter Marie again in her Ferrari, ostensibly to rescue her "lover," but really to rub his nose still further in the mess he has made of his life. While Abe fumes about his replacement at work by cousin Justin, "a fucking moron," Marie takes the younger man's part, and it rapidly becomes clear, as Abe surmises, that she is "fucking him"—yet another reason to unload on the increasingly defenseless Abe, this time with physical disparagement: "You're out of shape; maybe if you worked out things'd be different." It all comes to a head at Marie's up-market house, where Justin (Zachary Booth) appears, buff and beautiful, from the shower with only a towel around his loins, and Marie licks at his ear, exposing him while Abe watches, stunned: "Let's show Abe life passing him by." We then segue to the dream scene set at Toys"R"Us (discussed above) where Abe asks for a store credit on his misplaced fiancée, and Jiminy directs him to his manager, a bruised and broken-jawed Mahmoud. It is Mahmoud, as a dispassionate deus ex machina, who delivers the most searing judgments on a completely wracked Abe:

> You have no sense of irony. You don't even really know what it means. I know you don't mean to be a total asshole like your father. I know that you are courageous and loyal in sticking by Miranda despite her deadly and contagious disease, even though you know she was never really serious about you. And she would have been far better off with your brother Richard, with whom she has so much more in common. Very good looking, isn't he? Abe, I know that life has been unfair to you, because it has given you every possible advantage, so your feelings of

inadequacy are endless and unrelenting. Your toy collecting: a reflexive textbook pathology of Western consumerist capitalism. But still, I am afraid I cannot give you any credit. No credit, no exchange, no refund.

What this sequence impresses on us is that, in *Dark Horse* at least, fantasy is the space not of escape and utopian wish fulfillments but of an unflinching articulation of the Real of antagonism itself: the fault line that passes right through Abe, where his hostility to the status quo, and the world's massed hostility against him, breaks out in tremors and savage existential quakes. It is in dream that Abe's condition comes most powerfully home to him, his every flaw and failing a repressed item of self-perception that his unconscious will never let him forget. Which is as much to say that Abe's deepest and most powerful desire is the old Delphic maxim itself—γνῶθι σεαυτόν [know thyself]—which makes of Abe's story something much more than a lampoon of the man-child as such, or a cheap satire of the man-child comedy genre (*40-Year-Old Virgin* [2005], *Step Brothers* [2008], *Failure to Launch* [2006], etc.), but elevates it to something almost tragic. Reality, in this film, is where self-knowing never arrives, blocked by rituals and fetishisms and mythemes from ever emerging; fantasy, on the other hand, allows truth to erupt in agonizing torrents of humiliation and shame. Abe pursues in his waking moments desires that keep him in a holding pattern of arrested development; his unconscious knows better.

It is notable, too, that fantasy in *Dark Horse* is filmed more or less the same way that reality is filmed; the stylistic gap we have noted in film after film, from *Dollhouse* to *Life During Wartime* (where Bill Maplewood still has his visions and Joy hers) is now closed. For in this film the point is not to show how desire punctures the edifice of the Real with jolts of subjective wish fulfilment but to ally the phantasm with truth itself. There is a sense in which Abe's fantasies are social events, not simply private or solipsistic; it is as if fantasy is held open to a properly dialogical sociality. So the style of these long and complex scenes is of a piece with the rest of the film, to clinch the truth that Abe, in his everyday existence is *already* in a permanent escape from reality to which his phantasmatic episodes call him fatally home.

Indeed, it would seem that Solondz's attitude toward dream sequences has gone through a significant change since 1995. No longer confined to jejune wish fulfillments or violent fantasies, these episodes have, since *Life During Wartime*'s several ghost scenes, carried more and more of the moral substance of his dramas. Nowhere is that clearer than in his latest work. The final segment of *Wiener-Dog* concerns the aging Nana (Ellen Burstyn), who has inherited the eponymous canine and rechristened it "Cancer." Needless to say, this is a study in bitter and unregenerate old age. Nana lives with her live-in helper, Yvette (Marcella Lowery), who is as scabrous and mean-spirited as her charge; they seem to feed off each other's bad temper. But in Nana's study, where she writes up a blank check for her visiting granddaughter, Zoe (Zosia Mamet), and Zoe's partner, Fantasy (Michael Shaw), there is a portrait hanging on the wall of herself as an unspoiled young girl: long orange hair, white dress, bare feet, gazing out to the future with a look of placid indifference. It is this very image that accompanies the old woman outdoors in what is Solondz's most moving and effective fantasy sequence to date. Sitting and weeping with her dog in the yard on a sunny afternoon by the new main road, a broken Nana is visited by the pretty apparition of her younger self, dressed just as in the painting, who asks, "What happened to you?" Soon enough, three further avatars appear, in mauve, canary, and peach, respectively, each of them a different life Nana might have led, if "you hadn't chosen the life you chose," as avatar #1 tells her. "That's you if you'd continued to study art. And that's you if you had married your true love. And that's you if you had forgiven your mother." Three more avatars emerge from the woods behind her: "That's you if you'd shown kindness to your daughter. And that's you if you'd learned to overlook others' flaws. And you, if you hadn't given up on life." But it is not over yet. "And here's you if you'd ever liked other people. And you if you'd ever liked yourself. You if you'd left bigger tips." And all ten of the unrealized images of Nana's lovely youth commence to chorus for the dying old woman whom they have come to gather in: "Everything has a beginning, and everything has an end." But she is awoken from her dream of these angelic debt collectors by the sound of a passing semitrailer.

This vision, at once so gentle and quiet, and so profoundly sad, is the apex of Solondz's screen fantasies. In it, the brilliant natural lighting of Bill Maplewood's park and of "Huckleberry" Aviva's rural sojourn is recaptured but filtered through a delicate tracery of green leaves and branches. The soft yellow-green hues of the foliage are matched by ambient sounds of birdsong and rustling in the underbrush. The vibrant orange of the girls' hair, and their pastel garments, set off the natural setting with a strong suggestion of Dutch or Flemish painting; the backlighting renders their identical figures otherwordly. The physical disposition of the blocking in the area—the girls appearing in an elevated ring around the sunken stage of Nana's bench—carries connotations of Renaissance religious art. We are, indeed, immersed in a painterly space invested with the abandoned aesthetic dreams of Nana herself, as if her greatest work should have been this late dream of her going hence. Against all the accumulated proscriptions and taboos established by Solondz's own aesthetic protocol, the image is beautiful, hauntingly so: a vision out of Andrei Tarkovsky or Sergei Paradjanov.

Of course, the moral lesson is as harsh and unredemptive as the image is tender and salvational. The greatest enemy and critic of the unrepentant old woman is necessarily herself, and each of these avatars is a regretful emanation of her own bad conscience. But rather than, as with Abe Wertheimer, allowing the dream to merge stylistically with the "realist" narrative passages, here Solondz permits the fantasy to flood the film with visual pleasure, the same pleasure we noted in *Palindrome*'s "Huckleberry" chapter and Dr. Maplewood's pastoral fantasies in *Happiness* and *Life During Wartime*. That this pleasure is here overdetermined by Nana's artistic passion (her house is crowded with serious art and

Figure 14. *Wiener-Dog* (2016): Nana's vision

books on the subject) is, one feels, a clear sign of Solondz's maturation as an artist, allowing the style to emerge from the content rather than being imposed on it arbitrarily. In any event, the whole episode is far too aesthetically satisfying to be left alone by the lifelong satirist, who rudely deflates it with what I now diagnose as the dream sequence's diametrical opposite in Solondz's cinema: the excruciatingly long take of distressing, uncomfortable, or simply disgusting reality. Here, the matter is appropriately enough all three of these things—a fixed forty-seven-second long shot of the dachshund descending from the yard onto the road, where she is squashed to a bloody red pulp by a passing semitrailer, squashed again by a smaller truck, squashed once more by a yellow sports car, and squashed a fourth time by a passing Mini Cooper. The hovering promise of resurrection and redemption is then parlayed into a grim joke when Cancer the wiener dog finally becomes one of Fantasy's animatronic works of recycled roadkill in an art exhibition funded, presumably, by Nana's blank check. Aesthetics are finally, inevitably, forced back into the realm of inauthenticity and meretricious commodity fetishism by the heavy satiric hand of the director who will not yet—not ever—allow himself the luxury of an unqualified moment of beauty or tenderness.

Those forty-seven seconds of Cancer's last stand feel a good deal longer than that. Her flattening by no fewer than ten sets of tires is allowed to run and run, and run, in a sequence shot that has aroused more ire and hatred from viewers than any other in Solondz's work. But rather than being exceptional, the excruciating held shot is a mainstay of the Solondz aesthetic ever since *Happiness*, from which viewers will surely remember the nearly unwatchable elevator ride shared by Allen (Philip Seymour Hoffman), the overweight IT nerd, who has just admitted to his analyst (Dr. Maplewood) his desire for violent sexual intercourse with his neighbor, and that very neighbor, the svelte and sexy poet Helen Jordan (Lara Flynn Boyle), up to the floor they share of a Jersey apartment building. For twenty-five endless seconds of a cramped medium shot, Allen screws up his courage to confess his feelings, lets it deflate, and casts around for more bravery, while Helen looks everywhere but at her traveling companion. That the shot is preceded by a twenty-second shot of them waiting together for the elevator, during which he finds the wherewithal to ask "How's it going?," and a twenty-five-second shot of

The Law of Diminishing Returns | 103

them walking along the hallway to their separate rooms (he says, "See you"), makes of this unendurable sequence a test of the viewer's ability to withstand the bottomless embarrassment and incipient shame of Allen's atrocious interpersonal skills and lack of all charisma. Solondz holds the shots far longer than another director would, forces the viewer to enter into an intimate proximity with the "ugly feelings" they frame, and indulges the horror so aroused.

The trick is practiced again when Allen and Helen finally hook up for a tryst in her apartment—she has caller-IDed his threatening sex call and invited him over to enact her self-disgust as a sexual violation. The look on her face when she realizes her predator is the creep down the hall alerts us to the ruination of her plans, though Allen is perfectly oblivious, and meekly prepares to do her bidding. ("I want you to fuck me," she has panted into the telephone earlier on.) But the energy of perversity has drained from the scene like pus from a cyst, and as they sit on either end of the world's longest couch, the mellifluous sounds of "Soave sia il vento" from *Cosi fan Tutte* launch yet again the vessel of Allen's frustrated desire, and his hand creeps, ever so slowly, toward the distant, frozen Helen. The shot lasts two eternal minutes, toward the end of which she finally speaks: "This isn't working. You're not my type." With this the entire subplot of their relations ends in a humiliating detumescence of possibility. The held shot is unbearable for the way in which all of the psychic and sexual vectors defining the space of their compresence rapidly collapse into nothing: all of Allen's hyperventilating sexual potency and all of Helen's self-loathing finally have no shared phantasmatic frame on which to hang together; rather, they misalign so badly, the only possible outcome is a mutual embarrassment so lethal it threatens to burn a hole through the film.

And here a key is supplied to the implicit relations between these deeply uncomfortable sequence shots of failed encounters and disastrous psychic pain and the fantasy sequences discussed above. Fantasy, it would appear, flourishes only in the absence of such relentless friction as these held shots expose, and when such shots take hold of the diegetic material, fantasy as such is strictly impossible. If I now describe Solondz's insufferable sequence shots as images of the *duration of the Real*, it is to emphasize the privileged relation such moments have to what is most riven by antagonism, most scored by the unsurmountable divisions and exclusions of social space in his work. And it is also to point out the negative relationship between such durations and the images of fantasy proper, which have no proper duration but warp time and space around crystalline nodes of the subject's immitigable desire. Between nightmarish durations of the Real and lurid screens of fantasy, the narrative proper unfurls, but it does so only under conditions ratified by these paradigmatic, disjunctive categories of Solondz's cinematic ontology.

Two other distinctive held shots from elsewhere in his oeuvre have already been mentioned, and their brief description here reinforces this point. In *Storytelling* the critical denouement comes through the agency of the revenging figure of Consuelo, who returns to the Livingston home late at night, after her sacking, and towels up the cracks under the bedroom doors before turning on all the gas in the house. This compressed montage has followed a cozy image of both parents and Mikey curling up to sleep together in the parental bed, "monster-proof" and adorable. But what follows it is the cinematic coup de grâce: a static exterior shot of the house, crickets chirping over the faint background noise of gas hissing, as Consuelo (the monster with a key) steals away in the night, and the camera rolls. For thirty-three seconds we are led to imagine the silent suffocation and death of the entire family, sans Scooby, who is in the city that night, and for four extra seconds the shot fades to an all-consuming black. It is typical of Solondz never to show a violent act but only its prelude or aftermath; here, however, the discretion of the camera observing the murder scene as it is actually happening from a safe distance outside does nothing to cushion the blow of these four deaths. Rather, in these clinical thirty-seven seconds the "soft death" of gas inhalation springs from us a particularly disturbing spasm of empathy for a group of individuals we have come to despise throughout the rest of the film.

And in the "Henry" chapter of *Palindromes*, when Aviva has locked herself in her bedroom in protest against her parents' determination to force the abortion of her gestating fetus, we are treated to perhaps that film's most upsetting single moment, in the form of another cruelly held shot. To this point, all of the overt antagonism has been between mother and daughter, with Mrs. Victor cajoling Aviva on her bed to "be reasonable: the baby has to go." She rehearses all the sensational possibilities of a premature pregnancy: deformity, mental retardation, the ruination of an adolescent life, and so on. "It's not a baby! Not yet. Really it's just, it's like it's just a tumor!" With all of this conflict in the foreground, Aviva's father, Steve, has assumed a more reassuring profile in the moral middle distance—until he makes what we take to be his more reasonable and kindly approach to his daughter's locked door. From behind it we hear, with Aviva's rising, hopeful face, an assortment of soothing paternal palliatives: "I know you're upset, and I understand. . . . Could you please open the door so just the two of us could talk? Honey?" But the rattles on the door as he tries to open it grow more forceful, and the talk takes a threatening turn. "I'm afraid if you don't open up, I'm going to have to force it open." Again we see only the door from Aviva's side of it; the acousmatic voice, growing louder and more intemperate, is filtered through it, with dawning shades of Jack Nicholson's turn in *The Shining* (1980). As a violent attempt is made on the door, there is a sudden cut to a close-up of Aviva's face looking appropriately terrified as the correspondences with Stanley Kubrick's key scene begin to mount. "Why don't you just open the door, and we can discuss this in a calm, mature fashion like adults, OK?," the panting voice shouts in a growing rage, Aviva now trembling with emotions of fear, betrayal, and despair. *"OPEN UP!"* Terror now imprinted on her face, Aviva backs away against the wall, to thunderous pounding on the door, the father's voice plainly raging now as we cut to a horror-movie close-up of the doorknob rattling in its place and back again to Aviva's face contorted in a piercing scream. But this straightforward genre pastiche, which (as we say) "escalates quickly," is but a prelude to the shot that follows on a sound bridge of the scream: a long shot of Aviva on her bed against the wall as her shriek suddenly cuts off to a radical silence—all struggles at the door stopping with the cry—and we watch her panting in animal isolation against the bleak moral night. The shot lasts a harrowing eighteen seconds, and what makes it so effective, so emotionally powerful, is the disjunction this kind of duration allows us to ponder, between the mise-en-scène (brightly lit pink wall paint, a pink-hooded bed lamp and pink cover on the bedside table, a child's quilt, a love-heart floor mat, and the pink-sparkled letters spelling out her name above the head of the bed) and the remarkable darkness of the thematic material—teen pregnancy and abortion, with a parental-abuse chaser. Although Aviva will face more spectacular horrors and challenges on her journey, we never again experience such shattering empathy with her situation, and this has everything to do with the deployment of Solondz's signature device of the held shot.

There is, however, one last such shot demanding our consideration, since it provides a hinge to the final part of our discussion and returns us to the overarching claims about "diminishing returns" in this cinema. It will not have been readily apparent how this putative dialectic between screens of fantasy and durations of the Real participates in that larger economic dynamic of dwindling returns on an initial investment, but with this last sequence shot, some clarity arises on the matter. And the matter is, precisely, excremental. It is also, prototypically, caught up in a disjunctive relation with a series of phantasmatic shots such that this entire episode serves as a culminating instance of the dialectic at issue. I am thinking, of course, of the most infamous tracking shot in *Wiener-Dog*, which we turn to after a brief revision of the truly euphoric sequence to which it is the coda.

In the film's first chapter, about the cancer survivor Remi and his new pet, Wiener-Dog, we have borne witness to the trials and tribulations of a childhood presided over by Gen-X parents who are more intent on their voracious egos than actual parenting. When father Danny (Tracy Letts) brings home the rescued dachshund for his son to help with his recovery, the dialogue that follows with mother Dina (Julie Delpy) is textbook Solondz dysfunction (he standing monumentally, she moving frenetically between kitchen and dining room):

DINA: Now who's gonna walk it?
DANNY: I'll walk it. And Remi'll pitch in too. You don't have to if you don't want to.
DINA: Damn right I don't have to, but tell me who's gonna clean up after it shits all over the living room floor?
DANNY: Remi understands. He's not a little kid.
DINA: He's a fucking survivor!
DANNY: His hair's all grown back. The doctor said it would be fine, as long as he keeps up with the blood work. And now he's got all summer to learn how to housebreak it. It's gonna be *good* for him.
DINA: Fucking asshole.

There follows a superlative single-shot comic vignette of Danny walking the dog the next morning, dragging the hapless creature behind him, shouting: "Heel! Heel! Heel! Heel, goddamn it. Heel! Motherfucker. Heel, motherfucker. Heel, motherfucker!" Further friction is generated first by the dog's constant distressed barking as it is locked in a cage in the basement, then by the need to have her spayed. Remi is throughout a model of patient understanding, while the parents boil and seethe in various postures of rage and indignation, their every gesture a self-serving hypocrisy. The boy is biding his time, waiting for the moment when he will be left alone with the dog he adores. It comes when, one morning, the parents leave for yoga in their red Mercedes sports car (as Remi puts it, "You need to do your body maintenance"). What happens next is sheer cinematic pastiche and guilty pleasure. As Claude Debussy's "Clair de Lune" plays on the soundtrack, we see, all in buoyant slow motion, a close-up of the dog on a skateboard, images of Remi jumping on and off the designer furniture and tossing a beach ball in the living room, and of the dog tearing open a cushion and spilling the feathers within—followed by a delightful homage to Jean Vigo's *Zéro de conduite* (1938), its exquisite dorm room pillow-fight scene. As Remi bounces with his beloved canine on the family sofa, a gentle rain of down and feathers percolates from above, as radiant an image as Solondz ever contrived of pure, liberated joy. It is fantasy transposed into reality, a perfect hybrid of dream and waking, hope and realization—a projection onto the screen of a young boy cancer survivor's most ardent wish come true and of cinema's utopian unconscious.

The inevitable sequel is swift to follow, on the heels of a long-held shot that signals not the unendurable Real but the post-orgiastic comedown of an almost postcoital stasis: Remi and Wiener-Dog, immobile on their backs in a sea of feathers. Lasting thirty-three seconds, the shot is really a formal preparation for the sequence shot shortly to come. Having ingested a number of Remi's granola bars, the dog finds it impossible to digest them and, true to Dina's prognostication, defecates all over the dining room floor—vast stringy pools of the stuff, dropped willy-nilly like toxic sludge on the polished wood surface. As Dina bends to sop it up with paper towels, Danny barks at the dog, "You see this? No! No diarrhea! No!"

The phantasmatic scene of youthful liberty has come up hard against the reimposition of parental control, which is experienced as a gag-inducing affect. But in order to establish that affective cancelation on the horizon of the Real, we need another long take, a sequence shot that

Figure 15. *Wiener-Dog* (2016): "No diarrhea!"

exposes its duration as a vector of excremental slime. We cut to what is already Solondz's most notorious tracking shot: a rightward dollying close-up of the curb outside, where Wiener-Dog has left her summary judgment on the domestic politics of the home she is trapped in—an entire minute of screen time, set again to Debussy, taken up by a loving, tender image of the dog's endless trail of wet, yellowy shit.

Here the law of diminishing returns establishes a clear resonance with the dialectic between Solondz's screens of fantasy and his "durations of the Real." For the dog is a gift, offered from parent to child, that keeps on giving in excremental dividends. From the priceless, world-altering miracle of her initial value—irradiating and redeeming the fragmented existential space of a cancer victim—Wiener-Dog has lapsed, completely, into the valueless substance of shit, thereby exposing the hidden inner core of her original value: the nothingness of Remi's parents' love. The repeated shots of excrement (which call to mind the dog shit in *Storytelling*) are a metaphorical "diminishing return" of that parental care, a fitting illustration of the worthlessness of its tired circulation in the domestic sphere. That they—and particularly the long-held shot of the curb—should follow the ecstatic, joyful episode of Remi's achieved fantasy only confirms the underlying satiric venom of this "duration of the Real" as an objective correlative of a loveless home and the malignant economy of the gift of shit that it shelters.

The Gift of Shit

At one point during his session with Dr. Maplewood, Allen admits that, of course, the unattainable Helen Jordan "knows I exist; I mean, we are neighbors. We smile politely at each other, but. . . ." This aspect of his frustrated desire only amplifies its fevered intensity and adds pathos to his mounting need to deliver his special gift: to fuck her "so hard that my dick shoots right through her and that my come shoots out of her mouth." We will return to Allen in a moment but not before reflecting more on this question of the neighbor. Freud's observations on the crowning Judeo-Christian commandment—the golden rule, "love thy neighbor as thyself"—in *Civilization and Its Discontents*, were not of the most sanguine.

> Not merely is this stranger [the neighbor] in general unworthy of my love; I must honestly confess that he has more claim to my hostility and even my hatred. . . .
>
> Men are not gentle creatures who want to be loved, and who at the most can defend themselves if they are attacked; they are, on the contrary, creatures among whose instinctual endowments is to be reckoned a powerful share of aggressiveness. As a result, their neighbour is for them not only a potential helper or sexual object, but also someone who tempts them to satisfy their aggressiveness on him, to exploit his capacity for work without compensation, to use him sexually without his consent, to seize his possessions, to humiliate him, to cause him pain, to torture and to kill him. *Homo homini lupus*. Who, in the face of all his experience of life and of history, will have the courage to dispute this assertion?[56]

The increasing proximity of the neighbor, especially in late modernity with its high-density dwelling- and workplaces, raises the stakes of Freud's pessimistic account considerably: the closer he comes, the greater my desire to destroy my neighbor's autonomy and consume his essence. Gifts, in this context, are sublimated forms of aggression, with the ostensible purpose of dissembling my hostility as generosity, and the ulterior function of establishing a debt and an obligation. Without gifts, indeed, the crushing multifarious presence of so many neighbors would simply liquidate one's well-being in volcanic eruptions of hatred.

But the polysemous character of gifts (aggressive, palliative) dates right back to an inaugural psychological experience that every subject necessarily experiences in early childhood: "The contents of the bowels . . . are clearly treated as a part of the infant's own body and represent his first 'gift': by producing them he can express his active compliance with his environment and, by withholding them, his disobedience."[57] "To give" has always and already to be construed as an act of anal aggression, and this archaic sense of the verb maintains a stubborn currency in the age of accelerating human density.

A pervasive anal aggressivity haunts even the most apparently selfless giving, the giving of oneself in the act of love. In his Eleventh Seminar, Jacques Lacan speaks of the collapse of the "specular mirage" of love: "*I give myself to you . . . but this gift of my person—as they say—Oh, mystery! is changed inexplicably into a gift of shit.*"[58]

In *Welcome to the Dollhouse*, Brandon McCarthy, having already revealed his more vulnerable side to Dawn Wiener, is overheard by her in the school corridor approaching a popular girl who has not invited him to her birthday party. His behavior and demeanor are markedly different from his usual thuggery: he is meek, humble, solicitous, for he has entered the aura of a distinct power dynamic, that of the successful schoolyard politician, where the working-class poverty he carries like a smell has no point of purchase. To his query as to why he was not invited, the girl—Cookie (Christina Brucato)—replies with a transparent falsehood about gender parity. But Brandon has come prepared for this humiliation and blindsides her with an early birthday gift, wrapped clumsily in a torn paper towel. The film cuts to a tight close-up of the gift as Brandon hands it to the girl, who cautiously peels back the paper wrapping in an escalation of suspense. Everything here points toward a literalization of the gift of shit: Brandon's crude sense of humor and emotional juvenility, the logic of revenge following the certification of his rejection, the looks of incipient disgust on the girls' faces, and the wet sleaziness of the packaging itself. Yet the gift effects a different kind of literalization—of Cookie's name. "I didn't eat my dessert at lunch today," says Brandon brightly about the crumbling chocolate-chip cookie in her hands. "I saved it for you." The boy's sensitive core is now dangerously exposed in the conspicuous form of his poverty, his sacrifice all too vulnerable to class misrecognition. "But Brandon," Cookie lisps to a chorus of titters, "this didn't even cost anything." She returns the gift and exits, to his deep shame, a cut that wounds the more deeply for being observed by Dawn.

This exemplary scene is both a performance *in nuce* of the transubstantiation outlined by Lacan and a primer on the place and persistence of this theme across the oeuvre of Todd Solondz. In a superlative double reversal, we first expect a literal gift of shit and watch it transform, miraculously, into a sweet morsel of genuine regard, only to see this confectionary gift lapse inevitably under the gaze of the Other into the excrement it always already was. Brandon's gift of himself, so unguarded and loaded with risk, in the form of an object that is an exact homonym of the Other's name—this elegant and economical pun designed to win acceptance and esteem—"*Oh, mystery! is changed inexplicably into a gift of shit.*" That the entire transaction is witnessed by the school's instantiation of social shit in its purest form—the friendless, loveless, abject figure of Dawn herself—is perfectly inevitable. Indeed, this transference is prepared for in an earlier scene where Brandon's current girlfriend, Lolita, surprises Dawn in the girl's restroom and, in an effort to reduce her rival immediately to her proper value, demands of her a dark offering: the true gift of herself. "You didn't come in here to wash your hands," Lolita snarls. "You came in here to take a shit." Dawn's nervous protestations to the contrary are unavailing. "Liar," Lolita returns. "I can smell you from here." Nothing Dawn does can divert her antagonist from her ruthless course, whose motivation is always clear: "You stay away from Brandon. He's mine." Forcing Dawn into the cubicle and holding the door open, Lolita underlines the merciless economic logic of her humiliation: "Leave it. I want to make sure you shit. I want to see it with my own eyes." To bear witness to the tautology of a piece of shit producing a piece of shit is to clinch the underlying rationale of Dawn's serial abjection at school. To Dawn's question "Why do you hate me?" the answer is plain: "Because you're ugly."

Nowhere are these dynamics explored in such depth and at such length as in Solondz's next film, *Happiness*, which remains today the greatest contemporary work of art conceived under the sign of anal giving. What is extraordinary about this film is how closely and expertly this prominent thematic strand of the network narrative, which threads

112 | **Todd Solondz**

itself in every plot and subplot, is aligned with the overarching aesthetic contract of the film itself; its meticulously controlled style, form, and "voice"; and its aesthetic politics as such. And it is the nature of this exceptional agreement that sheds the most revealing light on Solondz's efforts as an artist throughout his career, since here we find performed, to the letter, the nature of his aesthetic undertaking as an "independent filmmaker" in the age of late capitalism—to present us, while persevering with an ostensible aesthetic of light entertainment, with a gift of shit so offensive to taste and sense that it short-circuits our very conception of cinema itself and so makes possible new figures and forms.

The film's opening sequence, with Joy and Andy at the banquette in the cheesy three-and-a-half-star restaurant, rehearses the entire problematic with admirable economy. The two are, of course, cubicle neighbors in the open floor plan of the corporate call center where they both work. And in a later scene, the anonymous logic of their close proximity on the shop floor will be played for excruciating laughs when a weeping Joy—who has just learned of Andy's suicide—tries to remind her immediate cell mates who Andy was. (They end up trying to recall the name of Edward James Olmos, whom Andy might have resembled, if they could just remember him.) With workplace sexual frissons set at such an absolute minimum, Joy has nevertheless accompanied Andy on two or three dates, presumably out of pity or desperation; yet Andy has managed to fertilize the bleak, corporatized situation, at least to his own satisfaction, with the promise of his immitigable desire. We join the action just after Joy has dealt the terrible blow of her "thanks, but no thanks," and the sustaining social etiquette of their routine office courtship has begun rapidly to crumble. The in medias res opening specifies the very moment at which *"this gift of my person is changed, inexplicably, into a gift of shit"*—we are directly caught up, before we even know where we are, in the reversal of happy fantasy into the antagonistic Real, the sudden conversion of Andy's pipe dreams into their excremental remainders. The immediate result is an affective rush to the surface of certain fluid substances in the body: tears, snot, phlegm. Andy experiences his suddenly excremental value as an upsurge of wet, abject matters, which he is unable to control as they leak from his face, to Joy's discomfiting embarrassment.

Yet just as the situation looks certain to collapse into outright psychic disaster, Andy rallies with a surprising turnaround: the bestowal of a gift—the pewter porringer repurposed as an ashtray for the non-smoking Joy. What follows is a scene of dark psychological brilliance, for with the *objet petit a* now placed strategically between them—that "Gansevoort reproduction, Boston, late 1800s" collector's item, wielded like a talisman—Andy can restore the very luster that Joy has so recently stripped from him. As he watches her go through the motions of politely accepting the gift, thus reducing her power over the situation, Andy awaits the exact moment when, having seen and appraised the market value of the forty-karat gold-plate inlaid base, Joy is moved to announce her new state of debt to him, in order to strike the decisive blow.

> JOY: Oh, Andy. Thank you. This really means something to me. I'll always treasure it . . . as a token . . .
> ANDY: No, you won't. (Pulls his gift from her hands.) 'Cause this is for the girl who loves me. The girl who cares for me, for who I am, not what I look like. I wanted you to know what you'd be missing. You think I don't appreciate art. You think I don't understand fashion. You think I'm not hip. You think I'm pathetic, a nerd, a lard-ass fatso. You think I'm shit. Well, you're wrong. 'Cause I'm champagne. And you're shit. And till the day you die, you, not me, will always be shit.

One of the funniest lines in the film continues this line of investigation. Bill Maplewood has just returned home from a session with Allen (and masturbating over a teen magazine) and complained about his patients to Trish, who, when he refuses to tape their conversations for her to listen to, complains teasingly, straddling and kissing him: "How come, no matter how much you treat me like shit, I can't help loving you even more?" Appearing to treat the gift of the other as if it were shit, acknowledging her excremental value, is simply to play the game in a different way. When Bill tells his analyst, "Trish is good to me," despite their protracted sexlessness, what he really means is "Trish is worthless to me, knows nothing about my true desire, would leave me if she knew, is a nasty gossip and backstabber, and is politically reactionary." Bill disavows the truth with the language of sentiment. Trish's joking complaint is much nearer the mark. The more Bill "treats her like shit" (refuses to acknowledge her value as an interlocutor and helpmate, prioritizing their son instead), the closer she clings to the promise of happiness he

114 | **Todd Solondz**

represents socially (as breadwinner, intellectual, "good father," etc.). Happiness, in this film and more generally, is what the millionaire in Alfred Hitchcock's *Psycho* (1960) says it is: a matter of "buying off unhappiness" with money, the general equivalent, or, in other words, shit. Only if everything can be measured by the general equivalent, then we, too, as workers and conscripts of the social order, surrounded by its disposable commodities and sustained by their circulation, are by that definition shit also. Trish has internalized the excremental value system so intimately that, having bought off unhappiness with the shit of her husband's worth, she is happy to be treated by him in the equivalent manner—like shit.

The spine of the film's network narrative concerns the sentimental education Billy Maplewood's father offers on the subject of the ultimate personal gift—Billy's semen, which, as an eleven-year old, he is yet unable to give. Their repeated conversations about masturbation, penis length and girth, and finally rape, all orbit around the matter of ejaculate—Bill's, Billy's, anybody's—which thus assumes the place of the film's central, symbolic "excremental gift." It is, as a substance, the film's "general equivalent" and connects the central plot to the plot of Allen and Helen Jordan, Lenny Jordan and Diane Freed, Vlad and Joy, Pedro and Kristina, and so on. Solondz goes to particular lengths to establish this substance not just metaphorically and verbally, but very graphically on two occasions. The first of these is the notorious climax of Allen's anonymous sex call to Joy, a sequence that switches from a long take of Joy, to a split screen of Allen and Joy, and finally to a solo shot of Allen. It is once we are installed completely in Allen's charmless apartment (Joy hanging up once she realizes what is happening) that the money shot can appear: a moan of sexual pleasure followed by a truly disgusting close-up of Allen's "sticky milky substance" as it hits the wall in a wet, gelatinous slop and crawls slowly down. This gratuitous substantiation of the ubiquitous male gift, in nearly haptic detail, serves to underline the consistent formula: my most intimate offering is always, "*Oh, mystery! changed inexplicably into a gift of shit.*" This allows the closing sequence of the film—in which Billy finally achieves an orgasm and spurts his little gift of "dickwad" (also in close-up) on the railings outside his grandparents' Miami condo, only for it to be licked up by the family Labrador, Kookie, and transferred to its proper Oedipal destination (Billy's mother Trish's mouth)—to bring the equation full circle: the sentimental education is finally resolved as a discipline of waste management—what to do with the "sticky milky substance" that is wanted nowhere and yet must be given.

There is a particularly affecting line from Paul Thomas Anderson's contemporary network film *Magnolia* (1999), which serves as a gloss on the economy at issue. Rattled into a searching honesty by drink and the jealous ragging of Thurston Howell (Henry Gibson) in the bar where his beloved Brad works, Quiz Kid Donnie Smith (William H. Macy) articulates the nature of his pain: "I really do have love to give. I just don't know where to put it!" The difficulty in *Happiness* is similar, with the difference that this "love" is reduced down to its barest, excremental remainder, which is put, variously during the film, in Helen Jordan's vagina by a suitor named Huraki (or was it perhaps Vilmos?), in Bill Maplewood's hand and trousers, on Allen's wall, in Joy Jordan's vagina by Vlad, in Diane Freed's vagina by Lenny, in Kristina's vagina by Pedro, in Johnny Grasso's anus by Bill, in Ronald Farber's anus by Bill, and on Lenny's balcony railings by Billy. Even on the two occasions when the gift is ostensibly wanted, Diane is obliged to hear Lenny tell her he "doesn't feel anything" upon ejaculating in her, and Joy has to accept that Vlad has exploited their coitus to steal her stereo and guitar. Only Helen Jordan is allowed to articulate the principle of acceptance of this excremental gift; it is out of a sense of utter worthlessness that any person could willingly accept an aliquot part of the film's general equivalent as an expression of their value. "Nobody wants me for *me*," she tells her sister, but that's precisely because "I am nothing! Nothing! Zero!" Embodying the zero, existentially annihilating oneself, is the condition of acceptance of the gift of shit. Outside of this condition of reciprocity, the seminal gift directly "nothings" its recipient (as Martin Heidegger might say). "It's no use," Billy answers when his father asks whether he has come yet; "nothing comes." Allen gets it: "I have nothing to talk about," he tells Bill. "It's better I say nothing" to Helen, which is precisely what he does: "I know who you are and you are nothing. You think you are fucking something, but you are fucking nothing. You are empty, you are zero. You are a black hole, and I'm gonna fuck you so bad you're gonna be coming out your ears." Come is what is yielded to the void of the Other, an equivalent of the "nothing" of their value. To give it is "happiness," the coming of nothing. (As Dr. Maplewood tells his son, "'Come' can be used as a verb as well.")

The name we give to this gift in its full annihilating form is, of course, rape. "What do I know about rape? If only I'd been raped as a child," complains Helen, "then I would know authenticity." But Helen, as we have seen, cannot be raped. As Consuelo tells Mikey in *Storytelling*, when he asks what rape is, "It is when you love someone, and they don't love you. And then you do something about it." Quiz Kid Donnie Smith never gets that far, trapped as he is in the agony of "not knowing where to put it." The rapist knows where to put it: in the void he has assumed in the Other. He *does something about* his unwanted gift, gives it anyway. Johnny Grasso goes down fighting, refusing up to the last minute to accept the gift of Dr. Maplewood's metonymic white powder as the rest of the Maplewood clan fall under its spell all around him. Under severe pressure, he finally relents and ingests the white substance (spread into a tuna sandwich) that prepares him to receive the other white substance—the excremental portion—without his knowledge or consent. It is the critical sequence of the film, shot and edited in almost Hitchcockian fashion, featuring an extreme identification with Bill's point of view, plenty of fetishistic shots of the boy recumbent in his pajamas, and close-ups of the fatal sandwich. But however explicit Solondz has been with the come shot in Allen's apartment, he maintains a steely discretion around acts of violence, and we are shown nothing of the rape itself. Rather, it manifests itself later as symptoms of abjection: a spurt of Johnny's vomit deposited at the Maplewood breakfast table, and, critically, a terrible moment of inspection of his own stool in the toilet once back home. "Mom," he calls out. "There's blood in my BM." With this utterance, the circuit is closed: the gift of shit has been returned, and the rapist is outed. Hospitalized and subject to the probing inquiries of the police, Johnny Grasso is finally offered up to the most abominable act in all of Solondz's work, when his father shatters his son's merciful ignorance with the violent interjection "You've been *fucking raped!*"

The brilliance of the sequence shot in which Allen finally comes, and miserably fails, to rape Helen is how the empty rituals of civility and neighborliness ("Come in. Please, have a seat. Drink?") fatefully reappear to render any true encounter strictly impossible. On the one occasion when the neighbor seems willingly about to get her due, the gift of shit is blocked. Helen, who wants only to be raped, is incapable of projecting her fantasy onto Allen, as Allen is incapable of projecting his onto her. Instead, watching them sit formally apart on the sofa, under that frigid *nature morte* painting, we witness the intractable law itself: *there is no sexual relation.* (The masturbatory info-sessions, Kristina's disgusted revulsion from intercourse, Bill and Trish's long sexual hiatus, Joy's manipulation by Vlad, Lenny's nihilistic orgasm, and the preponderance of rape all convene on this point.) By and large in *Happiness*, the gift of shit is blocked, just as the postcards from his mother that Allen affixes to his wall with his semen are blocked messages of maternal care and concern, unanswered and removed from the sphere of communication. Allen's special gift is mediated only by telecommunications, relayed and diffracted by the millions of wires that thread together the names in the New Jersey White Pages and the network narrative itself as a spectral community nowhere present to itself. On the telephone he is the dominating rapist Helen requires, and she is the masochistic magnet for his criminal attentions; off it he is merely the ugly schlemiel next door, and she the sneering celebrity living in a petrified "state of irony." Telephony holds the entire film in a state of irony: secrets relayed, confidences betrayed, privacies invaded, and threats issued, all behind the protective cover of a phone and before the crushing disappointment, the excessive obviousness, the fecal reek, of a face-to-face liaison. The sequence shot of Allen and Helen's failed encounter is an x-ray of the blocked gift of shit more generally, the nonexistence of any sexual relation, and the terminal arrest of circulation that marks the culmination of the age of anal capitalism.

In their illuminating conversation about Jean-Luc Godard's *Weekend* (1967), Harun Farocki and Kaja Silverman discuss particularly the film's pronounced anal dimension, noting that shit is "a signifier of equivalence, but also . . . a signifier of excrement."

> In late capitalism, the commodity quickly gives way to "waste." The supremacy of economic over other forms of value leads to a dramatic diminution in the *kinds* of value any thing can have. It also leads to a decrease in the *amount* of value a thing can have. The value of the commodity must never be increased beyond the capacity of many to pay for

it, financially or libidinally, nor leave that many without the reserves for the next purchase. There can no longer be absolute value, only objects for which substitutes can quickly be found. With this serialization of the exchange process, the moment of enjoyment of each new commodity also becomes briefer and briefer, so that it passes for this reason as well much more quickly into the category of "shit."[59]

Godard's film gives supreme evidence of the shift in Western capitalism toward this kind of disposable culture of rampant consumerism, away from the more regulated corporatism of the 1950s and '60s. It is interesting to note, then, that the famous tracking shot of the traffic jam in that film was a key reference point for Solondz when conceiving his dolly shot of the dog's long trail of excrement in *Wiener-Dog*; the association between the two films is forged around a camera movement and the category of "shit." This phase of late capitalism may have peaked at the end of the 1990s, the very point that *Happiness* and *Speaking About Godard* were released. This was also the moment that *South Park*'s character Mr. Hankey first appeared (in 1997): the "Christmas Poo" who leveled religious and cultural differences into one mire of consumerism, mobilizing the ideology of the gift in order to secure an annual turbo-charged injection of disposable income and credit debt into a flailing system of economic peonage. But anal capitalism—the economic culture of disposable commodity production—came up against a historical barrier in the 2000s, with the popping of the dotcom bubble, the sewing of the seeds of the housing derivatives crisis, the escalation in structural unemployment, and the terminal decline of the rate of profit. These and other factors were experienced as so many blockages in the circuit of consumption, leading many corporations to rethink their very relation to circulation as such. What the new millennium augured was a transformation in the logic of capital investment, away from commodity production and toward logistics and distribution, and the consolidation of a global supply chain. Anal capitalism, experiencing a structural blockage of historic proportions, went to work on the plumbing.

Happiness was produced during the convulsive climax of anal capitalism's ability to squeeze profits out of middle- and working-class America, and it should be understood as among the most important allegories of that climax. It is such an allegory because of its specifically historical mode of insertion into US entertainment capital itself. Produced by Good Machine and Killer Films on a budget of $3 million, *Happiness* was infamously dropped by its original distributor, October Films, when that firm's parent corporation—Universal—balked at the film's pederasty and masturbation. Good Machine responded by incorporating a new domestic distribution arm that lacked any of the resources and "push" of Universal, which then got reinvolved behind the scenes with an under-the-table loan to the new distributor. This way the parent corporation could wash its hands of the film's content, and the "independence" of the production could play as a stand against corporate censorship, while profits could still be made and returned to Universal (in compensation for the clandestine marketing support) in the event of a good run. As it turned out, not even the notoriety earned by these events could bring the domestic box office of *Happiness* up to the level of its budget: it made only $2.5 million. This story raises key questions about the very nature of cinematic "independence" in the context of anal capitalism's paroxysms of accumulation.

At a roundtable for *October* journal held in 2000, Richard Peña, film program director of the Film Society of Lincoln Center, commented on the sea change wrought to US film production by the post-1968 watershed (marked abroad, not coincidentally, by Godard's *Weekend*) in which "one moved from what has been termed a structure of vertical integration [in the old Hollywood studio system], in which studios controlled production, distribution, and exhibition all the way down, to something now quite different, perhaps even more insidious, which is horizontal integration. A company like Bertelsman or Sony now has an enormous range of power [over the various independent suppliers]. . . . This is a very important change. It has removed the accent on large industrial producers and levelled the field, even within the mainstream cinema, to a number of smaller producers."[60] With the collapse of the old studios, an apparent democratization was set in train, leading to the de-differentiation between films made "inside" and those made "outside" the commercial mainstream, operating in favor not of maverick and countercultural film but of the bottom line. "Working outside the studio system is no longer a guarantee against interference and censorship. Since the majors dominate the distribution system, they also—in effect—control the independent sector."[61] The result is what Stuart Klawans (at the same *October* round-

120 | **Todd Solondz**

table) calls "a reinstitution, in a different way, of the studio system."[62] Smaller so-called independent production and distribution companies orbit like minor satellites the multinational giants such as Universal and Disney, effectively doing the work of vassals in managing the lower end of the industry but without escaping the economic iron heel, the anal compulsion, of the system itself. Horizontal integration benefits both parties in unequal ways: smaller companies take advantage of the exposure to media outlets operated by the majors; the majors draw innovative creative talent from the subservient independents, which, because they are integrated, never truly threaten the economic basis of the industry. Co-optation takes place under the guise of liberation, a fact that cuts both ways. As Michael Z. Newman puts it, "At the heart of independent filmmaking is thus a contradiction between the nature of feature filmmaking as what one observer calls an 'undercapitalized business venture' undertaken by passionate entrepreneurs, and the desire of the indie community to be aloof from anything that seems too driven by the values of business culture."[63]

The question is, of course, to what extent Todd Solondz might have understood his masterwork as having escaped the quandaries of this contradiction. After all, if the apparent vocation of the "independents" to offer something alternative and aesthetically valid turned out to be, as Peña puts it, "very much a false drama, because they're all part of the same structure,"[64] then it matters how particular films—especially this one, perhaps the sine qua non of the "independent" pose at the end of the century—advertise their independence in the formal and stylistic stances that they take. For, to the degree that they do so, they are in bad faith. The "anal" logic of excremental de-differentiation smears all products with the same filth of complicity. And no film, I venture to suggest, knows this better than *Happiness* itself. The decisive statement on its behalf was made by James Schamus, the film's producer under the auspices of Good Machine—possibly the most vibrant and important of all the 1990s "independent" producers, whose stable of directorial talents included Ang Lee and Todd Haynes—recalling the pitch that needed to be made to October Films to distinguish *Happiness* from just another "pederasty movie":

> You would be amazed at how theoretical our sales pitch was. . . . We did not want to sell controversy. . . . So I came up with a sales pitch, a theory,

> which went something like this: *Happiness* is a film about the conditions of production, industrial production in the United States. People said, "What?" Well, I said, the industrial production of desire. This is a movie about the fact that in America, we spend approximately one-third of our gross national product convincing ourselves, through advertising and through the media, to buy the shit we make with the resources that go into the other two-thirds of the national product. That's an astonishing dedication of resources, and it actually shows you how resilient people are, as a rule, in terms of not developing voracious appetites that feed capitalism. You really have to convince people, with advertising, to want all this shit. But I said that what happens is—and this is what the film is about—that you tend to produce too much. The system is producing too much desire. So you have these suburban families, American families, and they're out there sitting in their houses in the suburbs, and there's too much produced. It's breaking apart the codes, the signals, the institutions that are supposed to retain them. These people are the site of an industrial production that far exceeds their capacity to resist. That's what the film is about. It's about the overproduction of desire.

Schamus then goes on to say, "I haven't seen an article [on the film] that comes close, theoretically, to our sales pitch for the movie."[65]

So here is a film whose producers understood perfectly well not only that the conditions of late capitalism are such that an "overproduction of shit" is the horizon of possibility in which all culture must operate but also that the film itself—its thematic and formal concerns, its qualities and goals—is saturated by that very motif and is indeed "about it." But it is "about" the overproduction of shit not in any external, objectivized sense. Rather—and this is what truly distinguishes it and allows us to conclude our argument—it has so internalized the excremental qualities of postmodern cultural production that it *refuses to be distinguished from them* as a conventional work of art or avant-gardist statement might wish to do. Is this true, then, of the rest of the oeuvre?

There is no question that, for Solondz, the world of general commodity production is a world choked of its potential and generative of untold, pervasive social ills. This is a condition reflected on constantly in his work, from the boy Timmy's sociopathic fetishism of his Tamagotchi pet in *Happiness* to Abe's infantile obsession with action figures in *Dark Horse*, from Scooby's CD collection in *Storytelling* to Andy Kornbluth's posthumous remorse over his lost laser-disc collection in *Life During Wartime*, from the tasteless clutter of the Wiener household in *Welcome to the Dollhouse* through the bland objects and corporate finishes chez Livingston in *Storytelling* to the up-market décor of Helen Jordan's retreat in *Life During Wartime* or of Remi's family home in *Wiener-Dog*—this is a world held fast in chains of worthless stuff, "the shit we make." The "pursuit of happiness" boasted about as a national right in the Declaration of Independence has come to be exercised in an asphyxiating medium of excrement that permits no durable social bonds or moral tapestry of character to form beyond the blind compulsion to repeat and accumulate still more. In the interview conducted for this volume, Solondz reflects on the fundamental place in his films of "living in a consumer-capitalist society and the ways in which it is soul crushing and dehumanizing." Recalling the restoration of business as usual after the September 11 attacks, Solondz has said, "I'll never forget how [New York mayor Rudy] Giuliani answered (the question 'What can I do?') with, 'Go shopping.' I always felt that was such an obscenity, such a slap in the face of the dignity of this, an insult to the heart and soul and spirit of this beautiful moment. And what does 'Go shopping' mean? It means to insulate yourself from the reality."[66] What the phantom Mahmoud calls out Abe for in *Dark Horse* applies to so many of Solondz's films' personages: "Your toy collecting: a reflexive textbook pathology of Western consumerist capitalism." One of the oeuvre's most compelling presentations of the various pathologies arising from anal capitalism's rampant successes—the figure of Bill Maplewood compulsively popping jellied candies into his mouth—has a telling history. In the script, Solondz had called for Diet Pepsi as the product to be consumed—and here we remember Slavoj Žižek on caffeine-free Diet Coke as the supreme instance of the suspension of all content in late-capitalist consumerism: "all that remains is a pure semblance, an artificial promise of a substance which never materialized. . . . In this sense we almost literally 'drink nothing in the guise of something'"[67]—but Pepsi had other ideas. "Pepsi would never give us clearance. Nor would Coke," Solondz recalls. "When it comes to product-placement, I'm on everybody's blacklist. Nobody wants to give us anything. . . . All I can say is, nobody wants to have their product or their brand contaminated by this movie."[68] The blacklist is real, and visible in the exterior shots of the Toys"R"Us franchise where

Abe does his shopping—a digitalized blur obscuring the name of the store. Corporations understand that Solondz's cinema is so critical of, and inimical to, the very logic of "product placement" that any branded product visible in his scenarios is seen as contaminated, smeared with the excremental filth arising from his satiric homeopathy of late-capitalist consumerism.

And indeed, for this very reason—his exquisite sensitivity toward the pathologies of capitalism as a "way of life"—Solondz has deliberately eschewed the traditional solutions of both "high culture" and the avant-garde toward the commodity sphere. Neither turning its back loftily on the entire debased domain and recoiling inside formal gestures of purification and abstraction, nor seeking to desecrate the hallowed ground of "Art" itself through antipathetic thrusts of mockery and negation, his work treads a dangerously ambivalent path that can also be understood, critically, under the rubric of the "gift of shit." For what is his fastidious "left classicism" after all—with all of its decorous suavity of means, its simplicity and economy, its formal elegance and penchant for scrupulous minimalism—but a coating for a pill that, in any number of ways, mimics the excremental culture from which it emerges? Rather than reject that culture, Solondz's films *are* that culture, rearranged and dressed up in the vestments of industrially sanctioned propriety. We are approaching the most fundamental aspect of his mise-en-scène, profoundly connected to its interest in junkspace and the bland anonymity of suburban environments—namely, its astonishingly high doses of kitsch. From the eye-watering colors of the world of the Wieners in *Dollhouse*—Dawn's wardrobe of Day-Glo greens and blues and yellows, pastel floral print tops, and blue/pink onesies; Missy's bright pink tutu; the offensive sunflower panel wallpapering in the living room; the multichromatic vomit of their framed wall art; the anniversary cake—to the lurid nightmare of Abe Wertheimer's room (which he proudly shows off to Miranda), with its red polka-dot wallpaper, collection of Absolut vodka ads ripped from magazines, No Parking sign on the door (above another that reads "The Abester"), mounted replica of Oddjob's hat from *Goldfinger*, *Gremlins* poster, collections of figurines from *The Simpsons* and *Lord of the Rings*, and so on: Solondz's interiors are saturated by the mass-produced and ersatz. Think of Joy Jordan's bedroom at her parents' house in *Happiness*, Brady's in *Storytelling*, or Aviva's in *Palindromes*; think of Marie's sad

Figure 16. *Welcome to the Dollhouse* (1995): the gift of kitsch

little house in *Dark Horse*, Dawn's apartment in *Wiener-Dog*, or Trish's new ideas about interior decorating in *Life During Wartime*. There have been few more comprehensive depictions of the ever expanding suburban kingdom of that element once decried by Clement Greenberg: "Kitsch, using for raw material the debased and academicized simulacra of genuine culture . . . is mechanical and operates by formulas. Kitsch is vicarious experience and faked sensations. Kitsch changes according to style, but remains always the same. Kitsch is the epitome of all that is spurious in the life of our times."[69]

This kind of contemptuous shudder at how art degenerates, through popular reproduction and repurposing, into a generalized "simulation of nonexisting feelings," as Theodor Adorno put it,[70] is historically specific to a critical, early stage in what would be called the "postmodernization" of late-capitalist culture: its subsumption in the economy as such, the final erasure of any "critical distance" that might obtain between the work of art and the sphere of commodity production. It is a stance that has been maintained by certain conservative critics, like Tomas Kulka, even in the face of a thoroughgoing dismantlement of the regime of the "work of art" and its replacement by various strategies of curation, collection, performance, and citation. And yet the concept, and its intention, persist. We know, when we are listening to the sounds of Air Supply's "I'm All Out of Love" while Allen and Kristina slow dance in the chain restaurant in *Happiness*, that this is nothing other than the full, late manifestation of what Greenberg and Adorno meant by kitsch, just as we know that when Scooby blasts Elton John's "Island Girl" out of his stereo, it is only an ersatz, disposable mockery of something deeper that dare not speak its name. In both cases, however, there is not a "nonexisting feeling" lurking behind the kitsch song, but a powerful emotion that has no other way of expressing itself. Allen and Kristina, desperately lonely neighbors finally making the effort to connect in the absence of any meaningful social rituals, require Air Supply to contribute the poetry of their dumb encounter; and Scooby, unable to explain to his family or himself that he is gay, can only express the truth via CD. This mediation does not amount to an *invalidation* of the halting expression but only a detour of it through the commodity form, an alienation that cuts both ways.

It has been a persistent misunderstanding of Solondz's art that, through it, he sneers at and ridicules his characters, smugly showing us how mired they are in inauthenticity, so stupid and comical because of what they buy, eat, exchange, and value. But this misunderstanding rests on a failure to engage with the true affective basis of his work: the desperation of a subjectivity raised into kitsch as a natural element, for whom "genuine culture" has never existed, striving to articulate its needs through the only medium available to it. Listening to Dawn Wiener struggle through Chopin's "L'Adieu" in her effort to seduce Steve Rodgers is at once excruciating and deeply touching: she transforms the waltz into execrable kitsch, but in that transformation she also partially transcends herself, makes a move otherwise blocked to her as a subject of commodity culture. This is something that Solondz allows us to hear, again ambivalently, in the pre-title sequence of *Palindromes*, when Mark Wiener plays this same recording at her funeral. Dawn's "gift of shit," despite its radical absence of aesthetic merit, also carries the bittersweet taste of vintage champagne.

Solondz has always been aware of how dangerously close such depictions of kitsch subjectivities can come to lofty contemptuousness. The character of Toby Oxman, the filmmaker in *Storytelling*, is there to actuate this self-consciousness in the frame of one of his films. Toby's dilemma is that in showing precisely how Scooby is "the epitome of all that is spurious" in our culture, his portraitist will always be taken for assuming Greenberg's position on that fact: superior, mocking, and

126 | **Todd Solondz**

exploitative. He wrestles morally with his project in what is ultimately a posture of bad faith. The final screening of his work in progress, which the audience inevitably takes in the spirit of a cruel satire on the suburbs, is so powerful because of our focalization through Scooby, who suddenly realizes that as the "subject" of an arty documentary, he could only ever have been a figure of fun. Solondz's film frames what Oxman's cannot: the gap or schism between the form and the content. It is in the wrenching affect of the close-up, as Scooby watches his irreparable humiliation being screened in public, that Solondz indicates the critical difference between his art and the art of Oxman.

Indeed, the various artist figures in Solondz's work can be taken as figural "stations of the cross" in the hyperconscious passion that Solondz has experienced for his vocation over twenty years. From singer Steve Rodgers, interested only in how his resemblance to Jim Morrison will look on his first album cover; through Helen Jordan, the unraped "rape poet" who becomes an Emmy Award–winning TV writer; and Toby Oxman, the documentarian who approaches Derrida to do his narration and breaks every promise he makes to his subject; and Marcus, the young writer who thinks it's enough to reference his cerebral palsy to make a name for himself; and Mr. Scott, the novelist content to leverage his fame to fuck undergraduates; and Judah, the budding filmmaker who wants to cast a neighboring porn star in his first opus; and Joy Jordan, the singer/songwriter who can't sing or write songs; and Dave Schmerz, the screenwriter who knows he has to mix up the "real stuff" with all the clichés and crowd-pleasers—the *schtick*—that drive the industry; to Fantasy, the poor man's Jersey-based Damien Hirst ("Fuck Damien Hirst!") who repurposes roadkill as hideous animatronic revenants of whatever art was when it died: in Solondz's films, the artistic gift is always a gift of shit. Helen Jordan's excremental verse in her book *Pornographic Childhood* ("Now I'm here / Full of rage / Empty of fear / Did I do everything / I should / Welcome / Womanhood") does nothing to limit the reach of her celebrity, her friendship with Salman, or her sexual affair with Keanu. It is the guarantee of her success: shit wrapped up in an elegant black cover, a fabricated cover story, and a "timely" theme. It doesn't need to be read; nobody will read it. What sells is the wrapping of trauma poetry. Fantasy's ultimate "redemption" of the eponymous wiener dog (now ignominiously called "Cancer" by the supreme misanthrope Nana), in the shape of a barking artwork mounted as an installation in the funky converted-warehouse gallery where Fantasy spends Nana's life savings on an exhibition, is the final twist in the long saga of Remi's father's gift to his son: the gift of shit, who began her time on screen unable to contain the contents of her bowels and ended it literally pulverized into viscera, tissue, and slime by ten sets of wheels, is here repackaged as a commodity you can hang on your wall, provided the price is right. A Tamagotchi in three dimensions, with a real bark, this nightmare image of excremental immortality is one of cinema's most punishing evaluations of the artistic function in late capitalism; it summarizes a career-long inquisition.

Solondz has squared his own circle, then, not by pretending to the august status of high artist nor by doing what any of these characters do but by remaining true to the promise of happiness implicit in the aesthetic contract . . . *in the form of its opposite*. Taking kitsch seriously, he projects the great aspirations for mid-century cinema—not just an art form but the supreme and emblematic form of its time—through the scrim of what finally undid them: television. For all the kitsch that populates his mise-en-scène as "content," none of it measures up against what remains his most persistent commitment to kitsch at the level of form: the square-framed, jingle-ridden, genre-driven, and purely conventional cinematography, scoring, editing styles, and color palettes of 1970s and 1980s American network television. If Perry Anderson is right to say that of all the technological conditions of the postmodern turn none was as instrumental as the spread of color TV,[71] then cinema's first reaction—nostalgia film, shooting the past in the styles appropriate to the era—was only an initial phase of adaptation to the new reality, whose distant sequel, the full cinematization of television itself through steaming and the digital turn, was an inevitable development. What has never yet been properly theorized is the partial appropriation of "classic" televisual tropes and devices to cinema proper, which is precisely the formal solution Solondz was fortunate enough to discover while formatting *Happiness* for the big screen. As has been frequently observed, *Happiness* and its sequels evince more that "just an interest in and appeal to a television sensibility"; they "exploit specific narrative elements of the form as a way of plugging viewers into an otherwise nebulous narrative order. In the situation comedy, . . . narrative action

128 | **Todd Solondz**

is merely a structure to support a series of jokes, product placements and public service announcements. . . . Sitcoms are designed to deliver messages, not catharsis or clarification, and are driven by inevitability, not revelation or intrigue. Like sitcoms, Solondz's scenes are episodic and self-contained."[72] More than that, the films' sound design and musical scoring—with their colorful "tags" and themes, the exaggerated color palettes, the ruthlessly efficient shot/reverse-shot editing for scenes of dialogue, the chronotopic monotony, the very structuration of so much of the drama around familial and domestic situations—all contribute to an inescapable sense that this is a cinema explicitly modeled on the form specific to commercial prime-time television. His compositions rarely attend to much beyond the foursquare aspect ratio of a 1977 color TV set, and the rhythm and pitch of so much of his dialogue falls right into line. Solondz acknowledges as much in the interview given for this volume: "I like sometimes imagining that the audience is watching a medical series or a sitcom, something on TV, that it's as if you might be watching something on TV, with all the conventions and formulas and narrative tropes and so forth, . . . in some ways to seduce the audience into that sense of familiarity."

With this admission, what we have been calling his "left classicism" comes sharply into focus—not as a reclamation and recalibration of the classical continuity narrative system of the Studio Era but of the industrial cookie cutter that churned out shows like *The Brady Bunch*, *Happy Days*, and *All In the Family*. The sitcom is the chosen vessel for Solondz's "gift of shit," a solution that has the truly unexpected result of turning it inside out. While Helen Jordan wraps her trash in the seductive cladding of a clothbound volume of serious poetry, Solondz has learned to package his profoundly serious "sad comedies" about the existential conditions of life under senile capitalism in the form of a network TV sitcom.

The law of diminishing returns now comes full circle, as a way of thinking critically about the immanent disappointment of every serial, every repetitious formula and catchphrase—which is to say, the nature of commodity culture itself, whose innermost temporal essence the sitcom somehow captures very exactly (as Harold Ramis's masterpiece *Groundhog Day* [1993] also realized). And a way of thinking, too, about the passing out of use value of the "gift of shit" itself as a

The Law of Diminishing Returns | 129

critical ideologeme for a number of works in the late 1990s, once the structural and macroeconomic realignments of the 2000s had settled into place. For as with every such formal or tropological solution to an overarching social and cultural contradiction—in this case, that our "freedom" is being lived as an enslavement to the universe of shit—subsequent historical transformation, however subtle or impalpable in its immediate effects, always renders aesthetic answers obsolete or at best compromised. They cease to be felt as the canny inventions they had been only yesterday, when Bill Clinton was president and the rate of profit was up over 20 percent. The ingenious thing about the application of the law of diminishing returns to this critical artistic trope is that it acknowledges the historicity of all cultural production and anything that aspires to the condition of art, since it rounds upon what is perhaps Solondz's most remarkable aesthetic feat—the planning and execution of *Happiness* as the apogee of a gift of shit—and shows that it, too, is subject to the same universal law.

On this point it must be remembered that of all his films, *Happiness* was the most audacious and "suicidal" in a purely economic sense. Having reaped an enviable 600 percent return on the budget for *Welcome to the Dollhouse*, Solondz made an inspired assessment of the opportunity with which this windfall had presented him. Clearly he could leverage the success of his auspicious teen movie and work his way up to being a new Harold Ramis or Woody Allen. "I always thought I would have a career in Hollywood," he says in the interview that follows, "that I would make movies that pleased me the way so many Hollywood movies pleased me." Or he could take what would now be the investors' inevitable excitement for his next "property" and turn it to his own artistic advantage: to make the movie he would never be able to make again, because, having made it, the money would never return. That is to say, *Happiness* represents the crucial juncture in Solondz's working life—his *Citizen Kane* (Orson Welles, 1941) if you like—at which, with an unrepeatably big budget of $3 million and final cut, he could make the film that would cement his reputation. And like Orson Welles before him, he used this bridge to burn it.

The subsequent films thus describe an implacable trajectory that could well have been foreseen at the outset: a stubborn refusal to shift ground but to dwell within the furrow opened by the 1998 opus, with

130 | **Todd Solondz**

the inevitable consequence of a dwindling rate of return. Radical new moves are made, to be sure, formal innovations in casting, structure, and satiric reflexivity that would be the envy of many other artists. But these have remained curiously invisible to the market, and the critics, whose conception of this career's diminishing returns is confined to the common themes that play out across its arc like so many leitmotifs. The conditions of possibility of *Happiness* having proven unrepeatable, both personally and sociopolitically, Solondz's decision to remain steadfast within his elected televisual aesthetic, his "left classicism," and all the other formal commonalities discussed above, may seem merely willful. Yet in fact that persistence has allowed us to get a better understanding of the artistic vocation itself in the faltering age of late capitalism, in which to *be an artist*, to "do art," is to produce shit that nobody needs and assume a position that nobody respects.[73] As capitalism has shifted ground from the rampant commodity production of the 1990s and entered a new, circulatory phase of its protracted crisis, Solondz's perseverance with an aesthetic forged under a former dispensation sheds its baleful light on the age of logistics and circulation, because what remains the same is the nullity of value itself, in which (as Marx once put it) "not an atom of matter enters into the objectivity of commodities as values; in this it is the direct opposite of the coarsely sensuous objectivity of commodities as physical objects."[74] Value under capitalism is a void, a nothing, that feeds upon our very lives, including the value of artworks and films. Christopher Nealon and Joshua Clover argue persuasively that "it is not possible to conclude . . . that there is some kind of value external to capitalist value. Indeed, the division of the political and the economic into discrete domains is a fetish of bourgeois thought," a fetish toward which Todd Solondz has been scabrously skeptical.[75] In that case, the last thing we need is to consecrate and revere, to idolize or elevate, any artist or artistic product. No retrospectives, no award ceremonies, no lifetime achievement awards, no "living treasures"—the entire pantheon of our artistic heavens is comprised of egos predicated on their own void. What we need is a cinema, if cinema there must be, fully alive to its own contradictions and inner worthlessness under the spell of the value relation and whose ability to reflect on this sensitizes us in turn to our own mode of insertion into the same relations.

I want to end, however, on a rather different note. *Wiener-Dog's* culmination on the living-dead effigy of an incontinent dog called Cancer would seem to leave this oeuvre in a state of acute negation with itself: a despairing, albeit blackly comic, assessment of the prospects for artistic work today and of the fortunes of Solondz himself, recycling a trope first engineered twenty years earlier and thereby nodding savagely at the course of his own career. But this is a film, perhaps his only one, that houses an affirmative image of the work of art—indeed, uniquely, an image of cultural labor without any irony attached to it at all. Moved to pick up a family of immigrant Mexican mariachi singers hitchhiking by the side of the road, Dawn and Brandon first make small talk with them (which turns out to be not so small: "In America, so lonely." "And sad. And depressing." "Like a big fat elephant drowning in a sea of despair"). But later that night, in a cheap hotel room they all share in the middle of nowhere in particular, the singers pay for their ride with a haunting and beautiful air. An original written by Devandra Bernhardt for the film, the song—in plangent minor key, played with guitar and maracas, and sung in close-up by the young boy—does what all art should do: it makes flowers grow from excrement. From out of their poverty, their alienation, and their radical displacement—as a non-individualist, non-white, non-US collective—these melancholy entertainers tender their gift to a rapt and attentive Dawn Wiener (as Brandon shoots up in the bathroom), as if here, at last, was something worth more than money, more than value itself.

> [In Spanish:]
> The full moon is a body
> Filled with dead languages
> He comes close and I move away
> He fixes himself and I burst open
> You go newly wed and empty
> Celebration and tragedy
> Your death is a part of life
> That has yet to happen
> Elusive whistler

Notes

1. "In Conversation with Todd Solondz," with David Carr, https://www.youtube.com/watch?v=6ffj5XiWWjI.

2. J. J. Murphy, "Life During Wartime," j. j. murphy on independent cinema, http://www.jjmurphyfilm.com/blog/2010/09/17/life-during-wartime.

3. "Todd Solondz on Independent Film," https://www.youtube.com/watch?v =UNpIPar52cA.

4. Michael Roberts, "The US Rate of Profit, 1948–2015," *Michael Roberts Blog: Blogging from a Marxist Economist*, October 4, 2016, https://thenextrecession .wordpress.com/2016/10.

5. Joshua Clover, *Riot. Strike. Riot* (London: Verso, 2016), 151.

6. See Borys Musielak, response to query "On average, how profitable have the big movie studios been historically?," *Quora*, https://www.quora.com/On -average-how-profitable-have-the-big-movie-studios-been-historically-What -type-of-return-on-investment-do-they-get.

7. Anna Breckon, "Being Unlikeable: The Failure and Optimism of Todd Solondz," *Screen* 59, no. 3 (2018): 311–32, 313.

8. "WTF Podcast with Todd Solondz," https://www.youtube.com/watch?v =EKm7PE5bSZM.

9. "In Conversation with Todd Solondz."

10. "WTF Podcast with Todd Solondz."

11. Let alone lazy accusations of sexism, racism, and the like, accusations that he has written into his most recent film, *Wiener-Dog*: "He's such a homophobe. He's an idiot. And he's old," as the cool film students with "I Can't Breathe" T-shirts complain.

12. Representational spaces, or "spaces of representation," are what Lefebvre calls space "as directly *lived* through its associated images and symbols, and hence the space of 'inhabitants' and 'users.'" See Henri Lefebvre, *The Production of Space*, trans. David Nicholson-Smith (Oxford: Blackwell, 1991), 39, original emphasis.

13. Rem Koolhaas, "Junkspace," *October* (Spring 2002): 176, 177.

14. Marc Augé, *Non-Places: Introduction to an Anthropology of Supermo- dernity*, trans. John Howe (London: Verso, 1995), 93.

15. See Sigmund Freud, "Some Character-Types Met with in Psycho-Ana- lytic Work" (1916), *The Standard Edition of the Complete Psychological Works of Sigmund Freud*, vol. 14 (1914–16): *On the History of the Psycho-Analytic Movement, Papers of Metapsychology and Other Works*, trans. James Strachey (London: Hogarth Press, 1953), 309–333, 332.

16. Marc Augé, *Non-Places*, 34.

17. Koolhaas, "Junkspace," 179.

18. Orly Linovski, "Beyond Aesthetics: Assessing the Value of Strip Mall Retail in Toronto," *Journal of Urban Design* 17, no. 1 (2002): 81.

19. Quoted in Ben Walters, "Todd Only Knows," *Sight & Sound* 20, no. 5 (2010): 8.

20. This is obviously the brand, although, for reasons to be explored below, the logo/name itself is blurred out by a digital special effect.

21. In an intriguing personal twist, the letterhead on the company stationery features a zip code that directs curious viewers to a "Leonard | Solondz property experts" in Milburn, New Jersey. These are the offices of the artist's brother.

22. Koolhaas, "Junkspace," 176.

23. For the long literary history of this figure in bourgeois fiction, see Bruce Robbins, *The Servant's Hand: English Fiction from Below* (Durham, NC: Duke University Press, 1993).

24. Karl Marx and Friedrich Engels, "Manifesto of the Communist Party," in *Economic and Philosophic Manuscripts of 1844*, trans. Martin Milligan and Samuel Moore (New York: Prometheus Books, 1988), 209.

25. Ed Lachman, "On *Life During Wartime*," Criterion commentary on *Life During Wartime*, Criterion Collection #574 (New York: 2011).

26. Bresson and Buñuel are two notable like cases.

27. T. S. Eliot, "The Function of Criticism," *The Selected Prose of T. S. Eliot*, ed. Frank Kermode (London: Faber & Faber, 1975), 70.

28. The exquisite Terrence Davies and the redoubtable Ken Loach supply a non-American coordinate for this intriguing category.

29. See Jeffrey Sconce, "Irony, Nihilism, and the New American 'Smart' Film," *Screen* 43, no. 4 (2002): 350.

30. This is the point to note that, despite his avowed enthusiasm for this kind of work, Solondz's cinema "does not take the form of queer, trash, or bad-taste filmmakers who revel in their association with all that is culturally denigrated. His engagement with failure does not fall into the ironic and celebratory tradition of being 'so bad it's good.'" See Breckon, "Being Unlikeable," 312.

31. See Jay David Bolter and Richard Grusin, *Remediation: Understanding New Media* (Cambridge: MIT Press, 2000), 20–50.

32. Lauren Berlant, "A Properly Political Concept of Love: Three Approaches in Ten Pages," *Cultural Anthropology* 26, no. 4 (2011): 689.

33. Jacques Lacan, *Seminar XI*; see Slavoj Žižek, *The Sublime Object of Ideology* (London: Verso, 2008), 204.

34. Walter Benjamin, "Fate and Character," in *One-Way Street and Other Writings*, trans. Edmund Jephcott and Kingsley Shorter (London: Verso, 1992), 130.

35. Haynes's film is then referenced by Solondz in the Oregon dorm room of Billy Maplewood in *Life During Wartime*, where a poster for it conspicuously adorns a wall, both repaying the compliment and speaking to the casting agenda in that film.

36. "Gelber's naturalistic performance means that he disappears into the character to such a degree that it may seem as if the actor himself is as bereft of personality and appeal as the character he plays. Depriving Abe of the star power, narcissistic persona and comic style of performance that would allow his pathetic existence to register within the realm of ideality, *Dark Horse* leaves the white male privilege at the centre of Abe's suffering without the camouflage of charisma." Breckon, "Being Unlikeable," 315.

37. Friedrich Nietzsche, *Thus Spoke Zarathustra: A Book for Everyone and No One*, trans. R. J. Hollingdale (Harmondsworth: Penguin, 1971), 237.

38. Ibid., 237–38.

39. Frederich Nietzsche, *Ecce Homo*, "Why I Am So Clever," #10, in *On the Genealogy of Morals and Ecce Homo*, trans. Walter Kaufmann and R. J. Hollingdale (New York: Vintage, 1969), 258. See also Nietzsche, *The Gay Science*, #276, trans. Walter Kaufmann (New York: Vintage, 1974), 223.

40. Ed Lachman, "On *Life During Wartime*."

41. Roland Barthes, *S/Z*, vol. 28, trans. Richard Miller (Oxford: Blackwell, 1990), 67.

42. Solondz, interviewed by Xan Brooks in "Todd Solondz's Pursuit of Happiness," *The Guardian*, September 11, 2009, https://www.theguardian.com/film/2009/sep/10/todd-solondz-life-during-wartime.

43. Jonah Weiner, "Solondz Nurtures His Indie Cred," *New York Times,* July 16, 2010, http://www.nytimes.com/2010/07/18/movies/18solodnz.html.

44. "Life During Wartime: Interview with Todd Solondz," *Electric Sheep: A Deviant View of Cinema*, April 5, 2010, http://www.electricsheepmagazine.co.uk/features/2010/04/05/life-during-wartime-interview-with-todd-solondz.

45. Sigmund Freud, "Mourning and Melancholia" (c. 1917), *On Metapsychology: The Theory of Psychoanalysis*, trans. James Strachey, Penguin Freud Library, vol. 2, (London: Penguin, 1991), 258.

46. "Todd Solondz and Paul Reubens on *Life During Wartime*," *Off-Ramp* 84, no. 3, KPCC Radio, http://www.scpr.org/programs/offramp/2010/07/31/15703/todd-solondz-and-paul-reubens-on-life-during-warti.

47. See Ghassan Hage, *Is Racism an Environmental Threat?* (Cambridge: Polity, 2017), 29–51.

48. Interview of Ally Sheedy in extras to the Criterion release of *Life During Wartime*.

49. George Eliot, *Middlemarch*, Oxford World's Classics (Oxford, UK: Oxford University Press, 1998), 588.

50. Karl Marx, "The Eighteenth Brumaire of Louis Napoleon," in *The Marx-Engels Reader*, 2nd ed., ed. Robert C. Tucker (New York: W. W. Norton, 1978), 594.

51. Henri Bergson, *On Laughter*, ch. 1, sect. 4, trans. C. Brereton and F. Rothwell, https://www.gutenberg.org/files/4352/4352-h/4352-h.htm.

52. Gilles Deleuze, *Difference and Repetition*, trans. Paul Patton (New York: Continuum, 2004), 115.

53. Ibid., 371–72.

54. Jodi Dean, *Blog Theory: Feedback and Capture in the Circuits of Drive* (Cambridge: Polity, 2010), 121.

55. Alain Badiou, with Nicolas Truong, *In Praise of Love*, trans. Peter Bush (London: Serpent's Tail, 2012), 44, 47.

56. Sigmund Freud, *Civilization and Its Discontents*, trans. James Strachey (New York: W. W. Norton, 2005), 101, 103–104.

57. Sigmund Freud, "Three Essays on the Theory of Sexuality," trans. James Strachey, in *The Standard Edition of the Complete Psychological Works of Sigmund Freud*, vol. 7 (1901–1905): *A Case of Hysteria, Three Essays on Sexuality, and Other Works* (London: Vintage, 2001), 186. See also Anthony Easthope, *The Unconscious*, New Critical Idiom (London: Routledge, 1999), 73.

58. Jacques Lacan, *The Seminar of Jacques Lacan*, Book 11: *The Four Fundamental Concepts of Psychoanalysis*, ed. Jacques-Alain Miller, trans. Alan Sheridan (New York: W. W. Norton, 1998), 268.

59. Harun Farocki and Kaja Silverman, *Speaking about Godard* (New York: New York University Press, 1998), 87.

60. Stuart Klawans, Annette Michelson, Richard Peña, James Schamus, and Malcolm Turvey, "Round Table: Independence in the Cinema," *October* 91 (Winter 2000): 5.

61. Andrew Hindes, "Letter from Hollywood: How Happiness Won," *The Independent*, October 25, 1998, 16.

62. Klawans et al., "Round Table," 6.

63. Michael Z. Newman, "Indie Culture: In Pursuit of the Authentic Autonomous Alternative," *Cinema Journal* 48, no. 3 (2009): 16–34, 26.

64. Klawans et al., "Round Table," 7.

65. Ibid., 10–11.

66. "Life During Wartime: Interview with Todd Solondz," by Jeffrey Edalatpour, KQED Arts (August 5, 2010), https://www.kqed.org/arts/31536/life_during_wartime_interview_with_todd_solondz.

67. Slavoj Žižek, *The Fragile Absolute; or, Why Is the Christian Legacy Worth Fighting For?* (London: Verso, 2000), 23.

68. James Mottram, "Why Is Director Todd Solondz Returning to the Film That Nearly Destroyed His Career?" *The Independent*, March 28, 2010, https://www.independent.co.uk/arts-entertainment/films/features/why-is-director-todd-solondz-returning-to-the-film-that-nearly-destroyed-his-career-1926742.html.

69. Clement Greenberg, "Avant Grade and Kitsch," in *Art and Culture: Critical Essays* (Beacon Press: Boston, 1961), 10.

70. Theodor W. Adorno, *Aesthetic Theory*, trans. Robert Hullot-Kentor (Minneapolis: University of Minnesota Press, 1997), 315.

71. See Perry Anderson, *The Origins of Postmodernity* (London: Verso, 1998), 87–88.

72. Dean DeFino, "Todd Solondz," in *Fifty Contemporary Film Directors*, 2nd ed., ed. Yvonne Tasker, Routledge Key Guides (London: Routledge, 2011), 369.

73. Here, despite himself, Michael Z. Newman seems to have misrecognized Solondz's efforts. "Indie is at once oppositional and privileged," he writes, with *Happiness* in mind. "It asserts its privilege by opposing itself to the mainstream. It is antiestablishment like the avant-garde at the same time that it is bourgeois, serving a prime social function of maintaining status." The status and privilege

maintained by Solondz's work is, however, nil. Its participation in a mimetic kitsch excrementality is a satiric "plague on both your houses," whereby neither the avant-garde nor bourgeois elevation is consecrated or preserved. See Newman, "Indie Culture," 24.

74. Karl Marx, *Capital*, vol. 1, trans. Ben Fowkes (London: Penguin, 1990), 138.

75. Christopher Nealon and Joshua Clover, "Literary and Economic Value," in *The Oxford Research Encyclopedia of Literature*, ed. Paula Rabinowitz, http://literature.oxfordre.com/view/10.1093/acrefore/9780190201098.001.0001/acrefore-9780190201098-e-123.

An Interview with Todd Solondz

JULIAN MURPHET: Your films all somehow knit together into a singular, if not always totally consistent, world: articulated by topography, character, and temporality into an integral tapestry. I can think of literary artists who have managed this kind of feat—Balzac, Faulkner, even Stephen King—but I can't think of any other filmmaker all of whose films interlock the way that yours do. You say that this has not been deliberate, that it just kind of happened, but now that it has happened, have you had a chance to reflect upon it?

TODD SOLONDZ: It's true that it's a common enough thing in literary works, and maybe because film is such a costly enterprise, unless you have some sort of *Star Wars* or *Star Trek* set of characters that are going on a continued journey kind of saga. . . . I haven't really thought about this being a thing. What I've said about the process of filmmaking is that it is one of discovery, and self-discovery, and the more you do it and the longer you live, the more you have to express, the sense of understanding what impels you to go through this process, which isn't fun, but is nevertheless deeply gratifying at the same time.

JM: And you'd say that it's grown out of that kind of process, the fact that you like your films to sit in some kind of conversation with one another, that's been an appeal that's grown out of the process?

TS: As I say, it's not deliberate; in fact the movie that I've been preparing—and I think as we speak it may have fallen apart, we'll see—but this new project happened to have no characters in common with any preceding movies and is set in Texas. That said, like any filmmaker who writes his own material again and again, it's hard not to recognize it as a continuing exploration of where you've begun. You know the Isaiah Berlin essay about the fox and the hedgehog; I don't think there's any ambiguity or confusion about where I lie there.

JM: There are knowing references to other films and filmmakers in your work: notably, to *American Beauty* [Sam Mendes, 1999] in *Storytelling*; Linklater's *Boyhood* [2014]. Vigo's *Zéro de conduite* [1933] and [Luc] Bresson's *Au Hasard Balthasar* [1966] in *Wiener-Dog*; Todd Haynes's *I'm Not There* [2007] in *Life During Wartime*; and Charles Laughton's *Night of the Hunter* [1955] and *The Sound of Music* [Wise, 1965] in *Palindromes*.

TS: It's not, I think, often observed, but the ending of *Wiener-Dog*, when the dog gets run over, is very much inspired by *Mouchette* [Bresson, 1967]. And *Belissima* [Luchino Visconti, 1951] had a big impact on me, and you can see that played out in *Storytelling*. And there's a lot more of that in this movie that who knows will ever be made now—the Penélope Cruz movie . . . It's hard not to be in conversation, in some sense, with filmmakers that had an impact on you, and whether that's conscious or self-conscious, or unconscious, it's hard for that not to be taking place, because we're all so much heirs to that which precedes us.

JM: Some of the contemporary references, particularly the Mendes, tended to be a little critical, or at least ironic.

TS: Perhaps I have to plead guilty on the Sam Mendes reference. It is a case where there was a little bit of malice. You know, it was sometime after I had been doing my *Happiness* press, and Sam Mendes was doing his press subsequently on *American Beauty*, and it had been conveyed to me, I think, the contempt in which he held my movie.

JM: So it was revenge?

TS: I dunno revenge, but it was a little tweak.

JM: Of the contemporary filmmakers you can think of, particularly Americans, whom today does it not embarrass you to watch?

TS: This past year the movies that I particularly enjoyed were Ashgar Farhadi's *The Salesman* [2016]; I enjoyed this movie *Glory* [Kristina Grozeva, 2016], which was Bulgarian; *A Ghost Story* [David Lowery, 2017]; *Menashe* [Joshua Z. Weinstein, 2017]; I love *Phantom Thread* [Paul Thomas Anderson, 2017]. I don't know if people think I don't like anything; there are lots of things that are out there, and you just have to . . . you know, it's what speaks to *you*, and what feels fresh and provocative, and thrills *you* that matters. The year before, I loved the documentary on O. J. [Ezra Edelman, 2016], and I enjoyed *Moonlight* [Barry Jenkins, 2016] very much, and the documentary on [Anthony] Wiener [Josh Kriegman and Elyse Steinberg, 2016]. It was touching. There was a documentary *The Art Star and the Sudanese Twins* [Brett Kelly, 2008]. This documentary *Tower* [Keith Maitland, 2016], very moving, about the first mass killing in Texas fifty years ago. So, you know, I suppose this is a little bit heavier in the doc category.

JM: I get the sense that if one peels off all the blockbusters, of which there are far too many, it's actually something of a golden age for cinema now, at the lower range of budgeting.

TS: There is a lot to see; you need to know where to look. Here in New York, while it's true that some theaters have disappeared, magically there are others that have appeared, revival houses, with very good programming, and so I don't have enough time to see all the things that I'd like to see. You have to really organize. I'm not young; I can't just go off on a binge. I don't have that time.

JM: Do you have established relationships with other filmmakers, people that you're close to?

TS: I'm friendly with different filmmakers, but the people who are the intimates in my life are not necessarily filmmaker people. But let me see, who do I know? Terry Zwigoff, if he comes to New York, I'm friendly with him. I have different kinds of friendships. I don't tend to see people very often, and I hardly even go out at night, because once you have children you just don't go out. Not out of asocial-ness; I just don't go out. I can't.

JM: Telling stories seems to be one of your strongest motives in making films, stories with characters you believe in and feel comfort-

Interview | 141

able investing your time and energy in, as well as other people's money. David Byrne once called song lyrics a "trick" to keep people listening to his music, and narrative is sometimes a kind of trick to keep people watching movies. But I sense that that is not the case for you. I guess I'm asking about the distinction between form and content in your work, and whether for you one is more important that the other. Does content drive the form, or does the form you like to work in dictate the kinds of story you tell?

TS: I hear you, but it's sometimes hard to separate the two; one comes with the other, just as I teach, and I teach writing and directing, and the classes are virtually the same, because when you are writing you have to think about where the camera is and how you're directing and conceiving of this material. And as a director, what do you have to direct if you don't have a story? And for me, everything is contingent on the narrative; it's that kind of merciless motor, that you have to respect at your peril. And you wish you didn't have to and could just have scenes of things that interest you, but it is on some level ultimately an entertainment. And I think even Ingmar Bergman understood that—that you have to find a way to hook and seduce and entrap your audience in some sense so they want to keep watching. And you pull out whatever tricks you can. I think when people say that a movie was too manipulative, what they're really saying is that the movie wasn't *good* at manipulation. Because a great film is great with its manipulation; it's just invisible, so you can't understand or recognize the way in which you're being manipulated.

JM: You are definitely a *writer*-director, one of the more consistent writer-directors in the American tradition, and so a true auteur. Interviews with actors suggest that you are insistent on the rightness of the script going in to production. There is, I gather, little or no improvisation or ad-libbing on set. You are already fully persuaded by your characters and their arcs once you have finished writing, and the filming process is seemingly an effort to do justice to your vision. I'm interested in the "writtenness" of your scripts, and I want to understand your sense of the relationship between what you write and what you shoot and how you shoot. Do you ever get the temptation to just "see what happens" on set, or does the written word always have the upper hand over the production?

TS: I think I should bring a little bit of clarity here. It's hard, when people are talking about their work, or about people with whom they work,

142 | **Todd Solondz**

it's hard to resist certain myths that you are in fact creating if not already subscribing to. There are certain narratives that just feel right, whether or not they're reflective of reality as it was lived. And, particularly when talking to the press, there are different agendas going on. I've always felt, particularly when there's a movie coming out, that what is being said is all in the service of selling the movie, and you should be careful of what is being said at that time. There's so much that *can't* be said because of the nature of relationships one has to sustain in one's career. But that said, my scripts, I always live with the illusion that they're brilliant and am always disabused of that in the cutting room. But you need to have these illusions; otherwise you wouldn't go through with it. But I can tell you, for example, on *Dark Horse*, Chris Walken and Jordan Gelber *loved* to improvise, and I'm open to improvisation, but it has to be within certain parameters. You can't just blindly improvise; it's too costly, and it's not going to yield much if there isn't purpose to those improvisations. So there are definitely scenes that were enriched, made better by their improvisatory nature. And I mean this with no disrespect, but Mia and Selma, for example, were not as excited by the idea of improvisation as the others. So you work within certain parameters, and sometimes there is frustration. The thing I always say is that with children, the one dependable thing about children is that they know their lines, exactly as you have written them. And there are some adult actors who are good in this way, but there are many who are not, and that can be a challenge and frustrating. I had one experience with one performer in one movie where there is a speech, and this actor/tress (OK, I don't want to give anything away), but their job as I see it is to know their lines! And after every take, a few lines into it—all right, *she*—she would stumble and apologize ("Gee, I don't know what's going on!"), and so I shouted (sotto voce), "Maybe you didn't memorize them!" And I had to resort to cue cards, and that got her through the whole speech, and after we cut it all together, people said, "Who is that actor? She's really good!" So in the end I'm happy, but I'm also infuriated. But she's not the only one that I had this kind of crisis with. But that's your job, whatever the crisis is; I mean they call it a director, but it's really problem solving. You know, you try to surround yourself with people smarter than yourself that can help with all the different brushfires that break out.

JM: I should say that my question was not at all critical; I think your scripts *are* brilliant. What makes them stand out and stamps them with such an identity is the work you put into those scripts. So I can see why one would want to rein in as much of the improvisation as possible. Is it possible, by the way, out of curiosity, to see a shooting script?

TS: I'd have to go through, I mean I published a few of them, but I always publish just the transcript. And I've always felt philosophically, in some sense—that's why I never do commentary for my DVDs—I want the movie, for better or worse, to speak for itself. And it pains me, the idea—yes, I could include some lovely scenes, things that I love and miss and wish could have worked but didn't ultimately, a lot of scenes that are gone, but I never include them. I accept that it's kind of a death. I accept it and move on. It's like the idea that I would read a book and then need to see all the other five hundred pages of material that was not included. Nobody seems to pine for that when you see a book published. I feel like this is what I'm presenting and sharing with the world, and the rest is just . . . you let go.

JM: That must have been particularly the case with *Storytelling*?

TS: Actually it's funny because there is a third segment; it's about two minutes long. It's an epilogue, and I loved it. I actually had two epilogues, two versions—I shot one, and they gave me money to shoot another, and I loved them both! I was tormented and it was too much stress. What I did with my students is I shared with them the epilogue. I had two different epilogues, and they all say I should have included it. OK. So maybe I made a terrible mistake. But I had reasons, and they still make sense to me, but they were very painful decisions to make, because I loved both of them in different ways. But I had concerns and worries, and it's hard to explain, because I'm speaking in the abstract here. So it was hard to let go of that stuff. It's always hard. There isn't a movie I've made in which I have not written a letter of condolence to an actor, and said, "I'm sorry, I am, but I'm afraid I've had to cut you out of the film." It's a failure of mine as a director. I write scenes that I think, *Well, maybe I don't need it*, but maybe it's such a good scene that I could make it work in the picture; it's so hard to know in advance but . . . I feel in a funny sense, I'm very rigorous with my students, and I think it's helped me in a way [to] be a little bit more rigorous with myself, and not indulge in things that, just because you like something, is not enough reason for it to be there, and that's very hard.

JM: A lot of other directors are releasing "Director's Cuts" on the DVD releases of their films. You're not tempted?

TS: Well, they're all my cuts. I mean, what am I going to do, the "Director's Other Cut he was thinking of, but didn't" . . . ? No, these are the cuts; nobody forced me to remove anything from any of these movies. And in fact, in *Storytelling* I actually had in the contract that—because I knew that the material was going to be a little bit rough; I anticipated that—it would be allowed to incorporate bleeps or boxes (audio or image) in order to procure an R rating here. And I did that because I didn't want to put myself into the position where I would actually have to remove something that I wanted. I would rather an audience know what I intended, because if it's not there, then they'll never know. So this way, when I have my sex scene with the teacher and the student, black on white, in America [not in Australia] there's a big red box covering up the sex . . . and I take pride in that, because it's the only studio movie ever made with that in it! On a certain level, it heightens the forbiddenness and the political censoriousness of the scene, so I feel ultimately bad for all the countries that don't have the red box. In fact, the US release on DVD has essentially the director's version and then the family version. It still says, "Nigger, fuck me harder!" though.

JM: I think of you, mainly, as a classicist at the level of style (and this probably has something to do with your preference for certain composers in your soundtracks: Vivaldi, Mozart). With significant exceptions (that we can discuss in a moment), your compositions within the frame are relatively static and self-contained, very ordered and lucid; there is little overt play with depth or movement and little interest in what is off-screen; the definition is crisp and the soundtrack remarkably clear and easy to parse; shot/reverse-shot is the rule in dialogue scenes, with closer frame-ups during more weighted lines. And so on. There is a certain reassurance in it: indie filmmaker but without the weird camera angles and movements, without the self-aggrandizing flourishes and obvious technical tricks. There is a deadpan sincerity about it, an insistence on clarity, consistency, and steady pace. Can I ask you to reflect on this classicism as a consistent aesthetic stance across your body of work?

TS: Whatever you want to call it is fine by me. I think what you're getting at is that, because I feel that the text is already so charged, the

Interview | 145

MO that I give to all my departments is, I try—because I'm weak, but I *try*—to restrain. It's about pulling back as much as possible, to trust the text itself, to trust the context and the actors. I don't want to call attention to what's already there in a self-conscious way. That's the aim. So I like working with different people; it shakes things up. And what I would say ultimately is that, you know, obviously Ed Lachman and Fred Elmes are very accomplished cinematographers and have a big résumé history, but regardless of whom I'm working with, stylistically they all adhere and respect my sense of mise-en-scène, so to speak. People might say that I'm not "visual," but it's just that I don't think I'm very ostentatious about it. 'Cause there's always a sense that I have about where the camera is, and when it decides to move or not move, and what it's looking at, and all the elements of composition are always very important to me. Some cameramen will handle this more elegantly than others, but aesthetically they're all adhering to the same dictates, so to speak. You know, you look at something like David Lynch, and it's very rich and vibrant and saturated, and a very different kind of aesthetic. And sometimes I get people who think that's what I should be using because my stories are so "weird," et cetera, but I insist that it's a different animal I have here; it's restrained simplicity as best I can, because there is so much of a charge, I feel, already in the material.

JM: It works extremely well, I think, given that it's such a consistency across all your work, how hard you work with your DPs [directors of photography] to get it right, that there's this real tension between the style and the material. And the style is like a contract with your viewers, especially your returning viewers—kind of like a promissory note, that "I will be exercising the same kind of restraint as before," while delivering new and often very challenging materials.

TS: There's also even the element, I like sometimes imagining that the audience is watching a medical series or a sitcom, something on TV, that it's as if you might be watching something on TV, with all the conventions and formulas and narrative tropes and so forth, and so in some ways to seduce the audience into that sense of familiarity.

JM: This raises the question of the role of television in your approach to editing and composition and cinematography. You seem to prefer what I might call the ethics of the small screen, that domestic machine that we all live with: you prefer domestic and institutional interiors, and the ghost of the square frame, over cinema's large rectangular vistas, lavish sound stages, and location shooting (although *Palindromes* and *Wiener-Dog* do go a long way in that direction). And then, too, you privilege the logical editing style of cause and effect over art cinema's frequent dabblings with more illogical and expressive styles of cutting. Is this a kind of war of position against cinema, within cinema, in your movies, from the vantage point of TV?

TS: I don't know if it's an anti-cinema, because too much of what I do is formed by a love of cinema. And I do really love it. People talk about cinema as an art of dreams, but people don't realize that a lot of people—young people in particular, who are so used to seeing things just on TV and iPads and seldom go to the movies—sometimes people forget how powerful that can be. I grew up as a child watching TV—basically intravenously; I spent hours every day. And then suddenly, I think when I was fourteen, I just stopped cold turkey, I lost all interest, and ten years at least went by before I watched anything on TV again. And that's the period in which I fell in love with movies. But growing up, my experience going to the movies was generic as a suburban kid who was only allowed to see Disney movies, and the first movies were *The Sound of Music* and *Mary Poppins* [Robert Stevenson, 1964] and all the touchstones of this era, that's what I went to: *Chitty Chitty Bang Bang* [Ken Hughes, 1968] or *With Six You Get Eggroll* [Howard Morris, 1968]. I didn't see anything challenging, artistic, and so forth, ever. I didn't even know of that universe; I didn't grow up in, let's say, an intellectual, culturally sophisticated kind of world. That discovery came in my later teens, certainly when I went to college; that door opened up, and it was before there were Blockbuster Videos, so everything was projected. You went to college and you could see triple bills every night, you know, all sorts of things, and that's really where I got my education—where I first really experienced movie love and moviegoing in that way. But I was the "average American kid" in terms of what I saw. So when I look at, certainly, *Palindromes*, there's a reference from my family singers to the von Trapp singers, you know, and as I recall I think there's a kind of *Wizard of Oz*/*Alice in Wonderland* kind of reference going on as well. You know, it's funny, you go to college and you discover a lot more intellectually, and in all ways you're growing. And I was not a sophisticated kid, but you learn which are the great films, you're taught who are the filmmakers to see and these are the books to read, and it's kind of a recipe for how to live: you must do this, or you feel like inadequate or a failure. But as you mature, as you get older, really what matters most is what sticks to you, what do you really love, what it is that means something. Not what *should* you like, what *should* you love, but what *do* you love. It's always a charged question, and obviously it's played somewhat in that scene in *Wiener-Dog* that has the interview: "Tell me what movies you like," you know? It's so charged. Whatever you say, it's a minefield. "Oh, you like *that* . . . ? Oh, *that*'s what you respond to." You can see the sheer terror in the question. If they say, "Oh, you know, I like the Coen Brothers," it's *safe*. But what you *really* love, what really speaks to you—it takes time to learn to be honest with yourself. And if Julia Roberts movies is your thing, you have to learn to embrace that.

JM: And looping right back, do you think that you've learned to embrace that childhood self who was intravenously addicted to television?

TS: Growing up, certainly by the time I was somewhere in my teens, being from New Jersey was all so uncool, and it was the ultimate in, like, can't I just say I live near New York? "I live around the city." It took time till I could embrace and accept: that is who I am, that's what shaped me. It wasn't a childhood shaped by watching or reading sophisticated literature or film. It was a potpourri of all sorts, the detritus of popular culture, mixed with a patina or frosting of highbrow literature. So you learn to question, well, what was it that really affected you, what was it that meant something to you, and *how* did that mean something to you, how did you really feel. And then all of this ties in with your own life experience, it all becomes of a piece, and this is what you explore and try to create meaning from. As I would tell my students: make a movie that only you could make but not only you could sit through.

JM: On the other hand, of course, you have an insistent interest in the inner lives of your characters. There are powerful fantasy and dream inserts from the private worlds of Bill Maplewood, Scooby Livingston, Joy Jordan in *Life During Wartime*; Abe in *Dark Horse*; and Nana in *Wiener-Dog*. The "Huckleberry" chapter from *Palindromes* is also strikingly dreamlike and fabulous, probably my favorite single passage from your films (which also shows you can do great location work). You also like to move in and out of first-person voice-over monologues to yield glimpses into the depths of your characters' psyches. This dedication to the dream life and to fantasy pushes you to more experimental limits in your framing and approach to montage.

TS: If you're not approaching the inner lives of your characters, what are you doing? I can't put myself through this for a joke. You do the best you can to get inside, under the skin, to get something of the experience of what this character is feeling emotionally. If I didn't have an emotional connection with these characters, in each of my movies, if I wasn't moved by their plight, the movie wouldn't happen. As much as there's irony and a kind of detachment, it is concurrently, for me, always a deeply emotional experience. So whatever happens, at least I have that to hold on to. It means something to me, and the hope is others can connect with that. And I suppose I live by that cliché that when you go to a movie that you respond to, you feel that you are less alone in the world. As much of a cliché as that might be, that remains true to what I strive to do here. You feel more alive after going to a movie that speaks to you—movies can articulate things that somehow we are not able to in our day-to-day lives, even amongst our intimates. Often there are things that we can't express, so when we see it on screen, we go, "Ah, yes, I'm not alone in the world!" It makes one keep going.

JM: As an artist, when you're approaching shooting those sequences in particular, it seems to me you've got a license to be more lyrical, more poetic, to take a real departure from the way you frame or organize the rest of the film. Is that fair?

TS: It's not quite as analytical as you're making it out. I'm thinking also of a kind of rhythm for the movie, the way in which this scene can connect with that scene, and how it feels as the movie's moving along. The "Huckleberry" scene, I love that scene—that was my boy Aviva there, and that had a reference also to *Night of the Hunter*—and I knew I had to in a sense "go down the rabbit hole," and I needed something that could bring me there, that could express moving into another kind of reality. So I'm aware of what I'm doing, but I feel that it comes out of an instinctive sense of where I can go, what I need *here*. And things, if they feel poetic, in a truly poetic sense, if you're not careful it can feel self-conscious; it has to be grounded in the reality that you're setting up. To me, what's poetry is when the bully says to Dawn Wiener, "Why do you have to be such a cunt?" And she says, "I don't mean to be a cunt." And suddenly the word "cunt," the ugliest, vilest word, becomes a kind

Interview | 149

of poetry for these kids. It's always about the transformative nature of how you turn things upside down or inside out and bring a new meaning. That's the beauty that you strive for.

JM: It is beautiful; it does work. I was particularly moved that you reunited that couple in *Wiener-Dog*. To me, the end of that particular segment, when his hand falls on her hand in the car, is probably the single most affirmative thing that you've done. I feel that we've earned this moment, that we've been with you for such a long time, waiting, and, yes, we'll take it!

TS: It's very emotional for me and beautiful there, and unverbalized, that release. So yes. People say lovely things, people say mean things; it's out of my control. But I do think it's reductive to say, "Oh, he's just bleak," or miserable, you know. It just depends on the way that you look at these things. And I think it's not, well, "She can't watch the movie *Happiness*, because she was assaulted," or abused, or something as a child—but that's not true, because it's really about a sensibility. There are those who have experienced all sorts of terrible abuse—assault, or rape, or what have you—and they will come to me and embrace this film as meaningful; and then there are others who will be offended and outraged. There's no rhyme or reason to it. There's a project that will have me and three other directors, about Jerusalem. It's a nice little piece, I think it will be fun. You know, it's not a travel brochure kind of thing.

JM: I was going to ask about that, because what with President Trump moving his embassy, it's obviously a very charged time to be thinking about Jerusalem!

TS: I thought it would collapse because of that! But they told me no, it's hotter than ever! I should write another story and have it take place at the Trump subway station. Who knows where any of this is going.

JM: You've also demonstrated a remarkable experimentalism with regard to form and structure. *Storytelling* and *Wiener-Dog* are segmented into clearly distinct parts or sections; one of them is threaded together by the concept of a dog's travels. *Palindromes* is a fable told in chapters, whose lead character is played by eight different actors, one for each different chapter. *Life During Wartime* is a sequel of sorts, whose casting is a deliberate disappointment of the commercial logic of sequels in that all the parts are played by different actors from the original film.

150 | **Todd Solondz**

Dark Horse, a skewed romantic comedy, ends with the protagonist's death. This openness to experimentation at the level of form works in interesting tension with what I have called your classicism. You're certainly not as Brechtian as Lars von Trier, but there is an element in all of your work of aesthetic estrangement and confronting challenges to the default mode of cinematic perception.

TS: Well, it's not like a dogma. But I like to play with form, all the possibilities of form, and see if there are different ways that excite me in dramatizing the material. So, yes, I like to play with form but not at the expense of the material.

JM: It really becomes quite radical in *Palindromes*, where the commitment to the content was simultaneously a commitment to the formal novelty of the structure and the casting. The result was utterly unique and original.

TS: Well, it did take some courage. You know, I like to play, but not everyone wants to play with me—what can I say.

JM: Todd Haynes followed your experiment by a couple of years, and I was interested to see a poster for *I'm Not There* in Billy's dorm room in *Life During Wartime*. And I know that came about as a result of Ed Lachman's work on that film. . . .

TS: As the result of a few things. You know, you're doing a college dormitory room, where posters are signifiers, and then there's the reality of what you have access to, since you can't clear anything—almost everything's unclearable, particularly when my name's attached (you know, I'm on a kind of blacklist). . . .

JM: I wanted to ask about that. Is that blacklist changing at all? I noticed that in *Dark Horse* Abe could at least drink a Diet Coke, whereas Bill Maplewood couldn't in *Life During Wartime*. . . .

TS: That may have been true for *Dark Horse*, but certainly Toys"R"Us didn't want any association. Even though the material was fairly benign, it didn't matter, because I had a kind of reputation, what have you. And even, I suppose, without there being any taboo issues, the kind of sensibility, the kind of perspective, the kind of dubious look at consumerism, is probably not something that many people would embrace. I remember I was thinking of Andreas Gursky's photographs when I was at that shopping mall parking lot. But getting back to the dorm room, I didn't think that it was right that that kid would not have that poster and

Interview | 151

wouldn't put it there; in other words, it seems right for the character. But, then, it could serve in other ways. . . .

JM: It does, because that character is being played by a different actor than the one who played him in a previous film, and that's what's going on in *I'm Not There*, which is also what's going on in *Palindromes*. It's a nice bundled reference! Next I wanted to ask about editors. You've worked principally with a couple of editors: Alan Oxman for the first three films and Kevin Messman for the rest.

TS: Technically, it's two and a half editors, because I had two people working on *Palindromes*.

JM: Can you talk a little about these relationships and how important it is to share a sense of rhythm and timing in the editing room when making this kind of comedy?

TS: Well, it's really a question of a few issues. One is, the editor has a certain technical expertise. I don't know how to operate Avid or Final Cut or anything like that on a computer. So someone has to have that kind of expertise. And then, secondly, it's really a question of sensibility, and how I can get along with someone for so many hours in the room. So it has to be compatible on a personal level, but also, sensibility-wise, there has to be an understanding of what I'm trying to achieve. Now, that's not to say that I want uniformity of opinion; I like when my editors question some of my choices or ideas. Certainly when it comes to performance, it would be a problem if they weren't sensitive to the nuances that are present on the screen. So a lot of the time is spent, really, in discussion, in conversation about what we're trying to achieve and what we're trying to do. So there's a lot of discussion where no ostensible work is being done. But those conversations help us figure out how to move forward.

JM: Given that you work quite a bit with kids and some nonprofessional actors, how many takes are you generally juggling with?

TS: I don't know that there's a correlation between number of takes and kids versus nonprofessionals versus adults unless you're doing something maybe with an infant or an animal, where it really can get into a good number of takes, or letting the camera roll for a long time. It really just depends on the particular performer. With some it can be they get it very quickly, and then it's just diminishing returns if you do too many takes, and others take time to hit their stride. So there's no rhyme or reason to any of this, but we try to find a way. And, honestly, I don't ever

152 | **Todd Solondz**

really feel confident that I know that I have what I want when I move on. I don't trust my judgment until the minute I'm in the cutting room, and then I know instantly what I want to do. But when I'm on set I'm in a state of uncertainty, and there's a kind of leap of faith, and I hope that I have what I need, that it's not too much. You're always walking a line where you don't want to be too obvious, and on the other hand you don't want to be too opaque. It's always a red flag, if the crew is laughing, that something might be too obvious. It's so hard for me to know. I have a sense of what I'm looking for, but there are so many things going on at one time that I don't trust my judgment until I'm in the cutting room. And that's even with a monitor; there are just too many factors going on at the same time.

JM: Has working with digital—the Red One [camera] was used on *Life During Wartime* and *Wiener-Dog*—has that changed your approach to shooting? Has it alleviated some of that anxiety, because you can just keep rolling?

TS: Well, no matter what, it always costs money. You're spending time, and time is money on a set, so it doesn't make it easier. There are different kinds of issues that crop up with digital from what you deal with on film. I don't have the option of shooting on film, I just don't, and so I have to figure out how to make that reality work for me, as opposed to "Oh, if only I could have done it on film."

JM: I associate you with a certain kind of shot, which frames a situation of embarrassment or tension, and just lets it roll, well past where you might expect the cut to fall. Allen and Helen Jordan in the elevator, or on the couch; the gas hissing into the Livingstons' suburban home at nighttime; the repeatedly splattered dog carcass on the road outside Nana's house . . . The shot is held and held. Are these shots something you particularly want to realize?

TS: You're kind of approaching it a little bit backwards, because it's not like, "Oh, I've got an idea for a shot and now have to figure out how to fit it into the space"; it's just that, dramatically or thematically, I feel it is important to hold for a certain amount of time. I don't think it rivals what you see in Béla Tarr or Gus Van Sant, you know, but I hold for a purpose. But the idea occurs to me because of dramatic context and what I'm trying to achieve. Not like, "Oh, I am known for some long takes, and so. . . ." It just doesn't work that way.

Interview | 153

JM: Sure, but in relation to the kind of classicism I was talking about, these shots really stand out. They have almost an autonomy in relation to the otherwise pretty steady cutting of the rest of the films.

TS: There's a kind of—I guess the word is notorious—but there's a shot [in *Wiener-Dog*] of what the dog did by the curb that goes on for a long time. In the script it just says, you know, the dog, the curb is filled with diarrhea, and that was it, but going in I knew the music I wanted, and in the back of my head was the *Weekend* [Godard, 1967] shot of the traffic, you know, and I wanted to ride this out. I wanted the marriage of the scatological and the beautiful, and in the context of mortality, the impending mortality of this dog. And for me, if it were too short it would be a gag, but if it's something other, as it's played out with the music, which is one of those iconic strains . . . You want to bring a fresh context or meaning, so it may start out as maybe feeling like a joke, but then for me there's a kind of poignancy and heartbreak that can only be achieved in the long take. I don't know that anybody knew what the fuck I was doing. You know, I can't explain these things. I just knew what I needed, had to get it done; I knew how it had to be executed, but I didn't go into an explanation of what I'm trying to do. I just gave them the feel, the tempo of the shot.

JM: That one particularly works because it's hard on the heels of that ecstatic slow-motion Jean Vigo sequence of the pillows, the joy, and the modulation from that to *that* is really extraordinary.

TS: Probably that's one of my most joyful sequences. Just as you pointed out that the end of the second sequence is perhaps my most romantic of moments. But it's hard, I think, it *is* hard. My films are harder, I think, than I intend them to be. In some sense I feel like, yeah, I would respond to this, and so I'm thinking of the different pulls within the way you can respond, in dual ways or multiple ways, emotionally, to an experience, to a shot, to a sequence. . . . I think that this is why some people have such different responses. And so sharp. I don't seek controversy; it just seems to come to me.

JM: I'm not entirely sure you mean what you say there!

TS: Well, sometimes you hear people say they'd rather people hate their movie than just be somewhat ho-hum about it. Somehow extreme responses can validate a filmmaker's sense of self-value. But I'd take ho-hum over hatred! Really it gives me no pleasure at all to be hated.

JM: Many of your characters are amateur musicians: Dawn's piano, Mark's clarinet, Joy's guitar, Remi's flute. Then you've had quite a bit of music written for your films, themes and songs by Jill Wisoff, Robbie Kondor, Eytan Mirsky, Nathan Larson, Mark Shaiman, and others. Then there are the pop track selections, for *Dark Horse* and *Happiness* particularly, which grate rather pleasingly against the Mozart, Vivaldi, Debussy, Tchaikovsky, and Handel. The soundtrack is thus a very diverse, dynamic part of each film, full of different tones and moods, often in tension with what we are seeing. How integral is the music a part of the way you plan a film? Is it something you begin with, or that gets worked out later?

TS: It varies from movie to movie. I remember back on *Dollhouse*, I described an emotional quality I was looking for to Jill, and I was in a panic; she only gave me the score in the studio the day before the mix, so I was a bit panicked. But she understood what I was trying to achieve, with that guitar kind of thing. I had a sense of what I needed. But there are times, for example in *Palindromes*, I knew what I wanted, quality-wise, and I knew that Nathan would be right for it, and Nina Persson. And I gave them two pieces of temp music that I scored the cut with: one was from *Rosemary's Baby* [Roman Polanski, 1968], and the other was from *Valley of the Dolls* [Mark Robson, 1967], and that's what I gave them, because I knew the quality that I wanted. But then there are times I had to figure it out. I knew in the last one, in *Wiener-Dog*, there wasn't going to be one overarching score; each episode was defined musically in a different way. I gave Nathan some Scriabin piano études actually, as a source for what he gave me, which was so beautiful. And I knew the first one was Debussy, and the third one, I wanted someone to mimic Claude Bolling. And I just didn't need anything for the fourth one. I was sort of surprised; I felt it sustained itself and that music would have made things more self-conscious. So I just never needed music there. But I didn't know that going in. On *Dark Horse* I knew I was looking at an *American Idol* kind of soundtrack.

JM: Where did you get those songs?

TS: They were, I think, aspiring musicians who were trying to hit the big time. But I couldn't tell the difference between those songs in the movie and the ones that did hit the big time. That's why I'm not a music producer. They all sounded the same to me. What kind of pulled on me emotionally was, you know, this kid who—not a kid, he's a grown-up—

Interview | 155

it's hard, you're in your thirties. It's one thing in your twenties, living at home with your parents, you know, you're saving up money, but once you're, like, thirty, it's become something else. . . .

JM: And you should not be listening to that kind of music in your Hummer in your thirties.

TS: But that's where his head was at. He's still from, like, fifteen years earlier. An arrested development thing.

JM: It's kind of hard to deal with, all these lyrics about chasing your dreams and attaining them—keep trying and you'll succeed—and that's the one thing poor Abe can't do. That kind of irony is everywhere in your work.

TS: It's punishing! I've said one of my favorite scenes in the movie—and I could have kept it going; if I were self-indulgent I would have let it go on much longer—was the shot where he's watching the scrambled names of movie stars on the screen in the movie theater. It felt like something I could put at the Whitney, you know? In one of their little black video art projection rooms? If I let it roll long enough.

JM: It's so quiet! His voice, you have to lean in to hear it.

TS: You don't even *want* to play the game, but you have no choice. For me it resonates, the whole experience of being subject to the kind of—I don't want to sound grandiose, it sounds pretentious or pompous—but this is the subject of living in a consumer-capitalist society, and the ways in which it's soul crushing and dehumanizing. And if anything, that's the subject of not just my films but so many. I can't help but respond to this. I remember some years ago I was in Egypt and seeing big billboards, everywhere these huge signs of [President Hosni] Mubarak. And it's like that's the state religion. The way the Soviets had their thing. But ours obviously is Coca-Cola. They're all problematic in different ways. That's power, the way it's structured. So that's what I think every one of my films is in some ways reflective of, feeling the burn of that.

JM: It's interesting you bring up that scene, because I think it's the only scene in your films set in a cinema. And you've commented several times that people will predominantly see your films today at home, because apart from screening at festivals, they really only get released in the US, and in New York particularly. Does that change the way you think about them while you are making them?

156 | **Todd Solondz**

TS: Well, maybe I should change my ways a little bit, because, you know, I'm having trouble! It's always a challenge, every time. I'm always lucky, I feel, "Whoa, I got lucky this time." And maybe I've overplayed my hand. I don't know. You know, if I lived in France, there would be a system in place for a filmmaker like myself—maybe Australia, I don't know.

JM: Hmm.

TS: There would be something, whereas in the States, it's entirely market driven. And today everybody, because of the reshaping of the moviegoing experience—that people have TVs with a thousand channels and computers with a million options at every moment—the big studios still are profiting. But it's the little art-house guy that's being squeezed, the market is that much smaller.

JM: Obviously there are a lot of political ideas in your movies, but you don't make screeds, you don't issue treatises.

TS: Well, in fact my third part, the epilogue to *Storytelling*, was I felt, for me, a little bit, I want to say, didactic. It was playing my political hand a little bit too overtly, in a way that—well, you haven't seen it, so I can't really talk about it. But the material itself already contains and expresses a political point of view so that I don't need to put any signposts out there. Nevertheless, people will assume all sorts of things. So I take it and accept that I will be read and misread in equal measure.

JM: I think of it in relation to the effectiveness of satire. Satire is effective to the degree that it holds back, right? And it weds itself to a kind of moral compass without necessarily being didactic in terms of where everything should go.

TS: There's a moral foundation, let's say, or anchoring, but it doesn't moralize, it's not moralistic. In part, I just don't believe philosophically that movies—I think movies can change people but not in the ways they might intend them to. They have a sneakier way in which they operate on us. I subscribe to the old adage, you know, that Samuel Goldwyn said: "If you have a message, call Western Union." I'm there with Mr. Goldwyn on that. To me, the message is implicit, it's inherent, it's there; you just have to know how to suss it out.

JM: Nothing dates more quickly than a message movie; whereas genuine satire . . .

Interview | 157

TS: It's just not entertaining. They're not engaging, they're not challenging. And they're not interesting.

JM: You raise the question of how films change you. What a really good film does, I think, is change the way you see things rather than change the things themselves.

TS: It does. You can be a big reader, but is that going to make you a good person? If that were true, then it should be a law. Everyone should be required, if there were some kind of medicinal, proven results that we get from reading or watching movies. But that said, it's about the right audience for the right movie; they can find a kind of solace as well as an invigoration, a revitalization. Some people go to movies for other reasons, like you go to an amusement park and you want to be thrilled on the rollercoaster, and if it can't supply that, then it's not good entertainment. I don't worry about these things. I know it's a small audience; I'm just happy that there's any audience.

JM: Sure. But I do think there are several ways in which you're asking us, your audience, to change the way we see. One of the things you do is cast nonconventional actors, even some nonprofessionals, and there seems to be a somewhat critical stance toward the standard kinds of casting in Hollywood films. You've cast people who are disabled, with Down syndrome, actors who are maybe too old, overweight actors, and so on, actors you'd be stretched to call attractive in a movie-star way. Over and over. I mean, you've also cast Lara Flynn Boyle and Greta Gerwig and so on. There's a full range of human appearances in your films. Does that simply grow out of the material, or is it a sort of war of position against the way Hollywood asks us to see human beings?

TS: There are a number of issues. First of all, just because you offer a part, that doesn't mean they'll say yes. And then if you're working with someone who's not well known, you have in a sense the privilege of presenting them to the world in a way that you hope will make them *see* them, or experience something special through them. And those who are much better known in movies, you try to find a new way in which to present them. But actors as well, they want something fresh; they want to do something they haven't quite done before. So doors in that way are open to me. But it's not like I have some plan. I like to think "Who's going to heighten the charge of the text?"

158 | **Todd Solondz**

JM: I was very moved by the casting in *Palindromes*, and not only of the Sunshine family but of the various Avivas as well. It seemed like such a challenge to the way we're usually forced to look at people.

TS: In some sense, within the logic of that world, that whole Sunshine family would have been aborted by Ellen Barkin. Even as they go around killing abortionists . . .

JM: The irony does not stop!

TS: There is a kind of poignancy, without which . . . there's got to be some sort of tug on me emotionally. Otherwise it wouldn't be worth it.

JM: Norman O. Brown, in his study of Swiftian satire, used the phrase "the excremental vision." It seems to me that, like a lot of modern satirists, you have a strong interest in the human body and what comes out of it. Lolita holding the toilet stall open to watch Dawn take her shit; Johnny Grasso staring into the toilet bowl, seeing the blood in his BM; Consuelo scrubbing up the dog shit in *Storytelling*; the aborted fetuses that Peter Paul shows Aviva; the extraordinary tracking shot of Wiener-Dog's explosive defecation in that film. . . .

TS: I would say for the most part, for me it's aestheticized. Or there's something tactful, let's say, even, in the presentation, because I don't like ugly things that make me icked out. I have a different sense of what's icky from my next-door neighbor. Everybody's got a different issue about what's icky. But all those examples you're mentioning, if I think about it, in the toilet bowl it's like . . .

JM: Well, we don't see it.

TS: We don't see it, and it's clean. And even the tracking shot, it's got the music and it's very gently played out there. And even in *Storytelling*, it is an immaculate kind of home that's defiled, so you want it cleaned up. It's not like a kind of relishing in the disgusting.

JM: No, right, but it's telling us something about the body that most cinema doesn't want to tell us. Stuff goes in, and stuff comes out, and it does so in rather uncontrollable ways. And it's always because of the way it's aesthetically framed in such lovey, clean circumstances that the excrement makes its point.

TS: It's always aestheticized, and I don't think it would be presented otherwise. It has to be. I think the most disgusting thing I probably did was actually the sperm shot up on the wall in *Happiness*, with the

Interview | 159

postcards. It sticks, he uses it like a glue. I don't have rules about it, but there's something so outré, something so extreme, about what he's doing, and I'm playing, taking liberties here with reality, because I don't think this serves as an Elmer's glue, you know.

JM: [Helpless laughter]

TS: I'm presenting this, and it's so extreme. If I didn't think it were funny in its extremeness, I don't know, and its sordidness—for me the comedy is what liberates it from its sordidness.

JM: And that sets up the remarkable final sequence, where the kid's semen gets licked up by the dog and transferred to his mother's mouth.

TS: That is funny, but it's not sordid at all, because it's on a clean railing and everything is clean and nice; it's a different kind of context. So there it feels like happy juice, happy syrup, whereas in Phil's room it's like, poor Phil, it's so disturbing. . . .

JM: Your films often depict artists and their struggles with their work, its authenticity, the capital necessary to develop it, and the employment they must take up in the meantime. There are writers, visual artists, musicians, and, of course, filmmakers (played by Paul Giamatti and Danny de Vito), and in various ways, your films could be said to work as statements on the condition of possibility of art itself today. These are not altogether encouraging statements. In the act of making a film, a work of art, you are often driven to show how impossible it is to make a work of art. Do you think of yourself as a satirist satirizing the very thing that you do?

TS: Look I play with the whole idea of the artist; I can't help tweaking it, because it often flirts with a kind of narcissism, and a kind of vanity, and so that becomes material in and of itself. It's funny with all these strugglers. With Paul Giamatti, I only learned way after the wrap, after we had finished making the movie, but I didn't know he was actually *mimicking* me. I didn't know that he was using me.

JM: [Laughter]

TS: But I don't really see myself, the reality of my life is different, but I do like playing with certain expectations and conceits of the artist, and the trials, but also, once you start using the word "art," it's a very slippery word. And if someone wants to call me an artist, all right, whatever, but I can't call myself that. It just makes me feel a little bit—it just makes me cringe a little.

JM: I guess that's what's interesting, though. This intense sensitivity and almost a will to forestall or forbid that very identification of you goes into the way you make your films. You're very sensitive about not being caught out as pretentious, or elitist, but that's what generates so much fascination in your work.

TS: That one phrase, that's even more difficult to take, because what—I don't want to be caught out? Because, you know, I really *am* those things; I really *am* a pompous, pretentious person. That's why I don't want to be caught out! But I see, I observe; you know, art and poetry are found in ways that popular culture doesn't really know how to take in. You understand? There is popular art, you could say, and popular culture, and so forth, but I think anyone who's serious about what he's doing—if you're serious about it, there will be sacrifices of all sorts in your life, and, look, it is a *business* that I am involved in here. It's like, every day of the year they've got another awards show, prizes for every film and so forth, and of course the little boy in me, the child in me, says, "Yes, I won a prize," and I can be happy like a child, but it is antithetical to what art is about. It's like having a painting and saying, "It won best painting in 2016." What does that mean? It's just anti-art, the whole idea of being in a competition, to win prizes. It's about business and capitalism and selling and the marketplace. But it's completely antithetical to anyone who's serious about their work. And yet this is the price one pays, on the one hand, to survive; you need this stuff, and then you become consumed with all sorts of self-loathing for even just a moment taking pleasure in what is devoid of meaning and is in fact everything your work opposes.

JM: And the character Fantasy at the end of *Wiener-Dog* is like a concentrated version of all of that, right? So desperate to get the prize; his whole idea about art is get the funding, get the recognition and fame. What really fascinates me about the way you approach *being* an artist—even though you may not want to be thought of as one—is how you occupy the field of kitsch and tastelessness, how your vision of suburbia is characterized by the inaccessibility of great literature, great art. And yet you try to construct artistic worlds out of a profound acknowledgment of and dwelling within that absence and its correlative, the plenitude of kitsch.

TS: You can grow up, as I did, with a certain level of shame or embarrassment. When you grow up you recognize, instead of attaching shame and embarrassment to these things, that this is the fiber from which your life has been woven. And so this is it! And how do you transform that in such a way as to have meaning for others? Kitsch is not inherently interesting, but only in the ways that it reflects something about the ills of society. And the ways in which it is used. Look, if I had grown up in a charming, quaint little cottage in the English countryside, my movies would be very different.

JM: It seems to me that art today almost *has* to be made out of that material in order to say something particularly significant about where we are. And that's what you're trying to do. And it's a high-risk game with an audience: you want your films to be beautiful in a certain kind of way, or have a certain kind of beauty imposed on them through the cinematic mode of production, but, actually, wrestling with kitsch is very difficult!

TS: Audiences, oftentimes they want certain experiences validated, certain emotions validated. And I am more out there to *invalidate*, or to question, to analyze, to open up. And that can make audiences angry, or disappointed, because I am not providing the kind of outlet that they are seeking. The whole idea that movie stars are so beautiful and so pleasing to so many people to look at in some sense is a kind of narcissistic experience that we seek out because we want to identify with those who are beautiful or those who are desirable. And the movies play on those assumptions. So my movies, I kind of want to have my cake and eat it too, because I do want, on some level, I suppose, a conventionally emotionally gratifying experience, and yet at the same time I do nothing but complicate that with whatever ideas I have in my head. And I think it's also true: I don't say this as some neat observation, but it's true that when I was younger, and for many years, I think until about *Palindromes* even, I always imagined—you know, I dreamed I could be a moviemaker, direct movies, write movies, be a filmmaker like that—I always thought I would have a career in Hollywood, that I would make movies that pleased me the way so many Hollywood movies pleased me. And it took me several movies to realize and understand that, no, I am not designed that way. And the things that I want to do to audiences are actually very different and in opposition to what Hollywood is designed to do.

162 | **Todd Solondz**

Filmography |

Schatt's Last Shot (1985; short)
USA
Director: Todd Solondz
Writer: Todd Solondz
Cast: Todd Solondz (Ezra Schatt), Cheryl Scaccio (Bunny), Kathleen Homic
  (Mother)
10 min.
High-schooler Ezra Schatt wants to go to MIT, but his failure to score a
  point in a basketball game means his gym teacher fails him. His girlfriend,
  Bunny, wishes he were more like Coach, whom he challenges to a one-on-
  one match.

Fear, Anxiety, and Depression (1989)
USA
Production: MCEG/Sterling Entertainment (USA), Propaganda Films (USA),
  PolyGram Filmed Entertainment (GB)
Distribution: Cineplex-Odeon Films (USA), M.C.E.G. Virgin Home
  Entertainment (USA), MCA Home Video (US), Metro-Goldwyn-Mayer
  (USA), Samuel Goldwyn Company (USA)
Producers: Steve Golin, Michael Kuhn, Sigurjon Sighvatsson, Nigel Sinclair,
  Stan Wlodkowski
Director: Todd Solondz
Writer: Todd Solondz
Cinematographer: Stefan Czapsky
Editors: Peter Austin, Emily Paine, Barry Rubinow
Composers: Moogy Klingman, Karyn Rachtman, Joe Romano
Production Designer: Marek Dobrowolski
Art Direction: Susan Block
Costume Designer: Susan Lyall
Principal Cast: Todd Solondz (Ira Ellis), Max Cantor (Jack), Alexandra
  Gersten (Janice), Jane Hamper (Junk), Stanley Tucci (Donny), Jill Wisoff
  (Sharon)

Format: 35 mm, color
85 min.
A neurotic New York playwright hopes to be recognized for his talents (even writing to Samuel Beckett for advice), but between his needy girlfriend, a sexy artist, his successful playwright friend, and his parents—not to mention the opaque impenetrability of his art—he finds success on his terms difficult to achieve.

Welcome to the Dollhouse (1995)
USA
Production: Suburban Pictures
Distribution: Sony Pictures Classics
Producer: Todd Solondz
Director: Todd Solondz
Writer: Todd Solondz
Cinematographer: Randy Drummond
Editor: Alan Oxman
Composer: Jill Wisoff
Production Designer: Susan Block
Art Direction: Lori Solondz
Costume Designer: Melissa Toth
Principal Cast: Heather Matarazzo (Dawn Wiener), Brendan Sexton III (Brandon McCarthy), Daria Kalinina (Missy Wiener), Matthew Faber (Mark Wiener), Angela Pietropinto (Mrs. Wiener), Bill Buell (Mr. Wiener), Eric Mabius (Steve Rodgers), Stacey Moseley (Mary Ellen Moriarty), Will Lyman (Mr. Edwards)
Format: 35 mm, color
88 min.
Adolescent misfit Dawn Wiener tries to navigate and survive the brutal world of junior high school and the malign neglect of being the middle child at home. Gradually an intimacy develops between her and her principal bully, Brandon McCarthy, but her crush on heartthrob Steve Rodgers and the kidnapping of her little sister make for complications.

Happiness (1998)
USA
Production: Good Machine
Distribution: Good Machine
Producers: Ted Hope, Christine Vachon
Director: Todd Solondz
Writer: Todd Solondz
Cinematographer: Maryse Alberti
Editor: Alan Oxman

Composer: Robbie Kondor
Production Designer: Thérèse DePrez
Art Director: John Bruce
Costume Designer: Kathryn Nixon
Principal Cast: Jane Adams (Joy Jordan), Dylan Baker (Bill Maplewood), Philip Seymour Hoffman (Allen), Lara Flynn Boyle (Helen Jordan), Cynthia Stevenson (Trish Maplewood), Jon Lovitz (Andy Kornbluth), Ben Gazzara (Lenny Jordan), Louise Lasser (Mona Jordan), Camryn Manheim (Kristina), Jared Harris (Vlad), Dan Moran (Joe Grasso), Marla Maples (Ann Chambeau), Elizabeth Ashley (Diane Freed), Rufus Read (Billy Maplewood), Evan Silverberg (Johnny Grasso)
Format: 35 mm, color
134 min.
The three Jordan sisters (Trish, Joy, and Helen) live very different lives in suburban New Jersey. Trish "has it all," with a husband and three children; Helen is a successful poet with multiple lovers; while Joy is a loser, working in a call center and failing at love. Trish's psychologist husband, Bill, harbors a dark secret (he is a pedophile) while attentively instructing his son in the art of masturbation. Joy leaves the call center when her rejected suitor kills himself; she then teaches English (as a scab) to immigrants in the city, where one of her students, a Russian cab driver, pursues her. Helen is secretly convinced of her own worthlessness and welcomes a predatory sex caller (her neighbor Allen) to rape her. Allen's other neighbor, Kristina, tries to get him to notice her and confesses to killing the doorman after he raped her one night over ice cream. The Jordan parents, Mona and Lenny, having retired to Florida, decide to separate, to nobody's satisfaction. Bill's rapes of two prepubescent boys eventually catch up with him, and the scandal erupts.

Storytelling (2001)
USA
Production: New Line Cinema
Distribution: Fine Line Features
Producers: Ted Hope, Christine Vachon
Director: Todd Solondz
Writer: Todd Solondz
Cinematographer: Frederick Elmes
Editor: Alan Oxman
Composer: Nathan Larson
Production Designer: James Chinlund
Art Direction: Judy Rhee
Costume Designer: John Dunn
Principal Cast: Selma Blair (Vi), Leo Fitzpatrick (Marcus), Robert Wisdom (Mr. Scott), Maria Thayer (Amy), Aleksa Palladino (Catherine), Mary

Lynn Rajskub (Melinda), Paul Giamatti (Toby Oxman), Mark Webber (Scooby Livingston), John Goodman (Marty Livingston), Julie Hagerty (Fern Livingston), Jonathan Osser (Mikey Livingston), Noah Fleiss (Brady Livingston), Lupe Ontiveros (Consuelo), Conan O'Brien (Conan O'Brien)

Format: 35 mm, color

87 min.

A two-part film. In the first part, "Fiction," creative writing student Vi sleeps with her cerebral palsy–afflicted classmate and attempts to impress the professor with her work. Her talent is lacking and she goes home with him instead, where she discovers a cache of naked photographs of her other female classmates. He proceeds to rape her while making her ask for it. She writes a story based on the experience, which is criticized for racism and implausibility by her classmates. Part two, "Non-Fiction," concerns a New York filmmaker trying to make a documentary about teenagers and the high school experience today. Settling on slacker Scooby Livingston as a suitable subject, the filmmaker begins filming much of the family's life. Struggling to get the tone right, he follows Scooby through the college admissions process. But behind the scenes, the maid is abused and finally fired by the family, and she exacts a terrible revenge, none of which ends up on the film within the film.

Palindromes (2004)

USA

Production: Extra Large Pictures

Distribution: Wellspring Media

Producers: Mike S. Ryan, Derrick Tseng

Director: Todd Solondz

Writer: Todd Solondz

Cinematographer: Tom Richmond

Editors: Mollie Goldstein, Kevin Messman

Composer: Nathan Larson

Production Designer: David Doernberg

Costume Designer: Vicki Farrell

Principal Cast: Ellen Barkin (Joyce Victor), Jennifer Jason Leigh ("Mark" Aviva), Matthew Faber (Mark Wiener), Stephen Adly Giurgis (Joe/Earl/Bob), Emani Sledge ("Dawn" Aviva), Valerie Shusterov ("Judah" Aviva), Richard Masur (Steve Victor), Robert Agri (First Judah), Hannah Freiman ("Henry" Aviva), Stephen Singer (Dr. Fleischer), Rachel Corr ("Henrietta" Aviva), Will Denton ("Huckleberry" Aviva), Sharon Wilkins ("Mama Sunshine" Aviva), Alexander Brickel (Peter Paul), Debra Monk (Mama Sunshine), Tyler Maynard (Jiminy), Walter Bobbie (Bo Sunshine), Richard Riehle (Dr. Dan), Shayna Levine ("Bob" Aviva)

Format: 35 mm, color
100 min.

Aviva Victor, a teenager, only wants babies. When she becomes pregnant by a family friend, and her parents force her to have an abortion, she goes on the road. First taking up with a trucker who deserts her after one night together, she drifts down a river to the rural compound of Mama Sunshine, who looks after a house full of rejected children. Finding her place in this Christian world, Aviva makes friends and tries to forget her ordeal. But when she discovers that the family is secretly involved in terrorism against abortionists, she becomes conscripted into the task of assassinating the surgeon who performed the termination of her own pregnancy. Eventually she finds herself back home.

Life During Wartime (2009)
USA
Production: Werc Werk Works
Distribution: IFC Films
Producers: Derrick Tseng, Christine K. Walker
Director: Todd Solondz
Writer: Todd Solondz
Cinematographer: Edward Lachman
Editor: Kevin Messman
Production Designer: Roshelle Berliner
Art Direction: Matteo De Cosmo
Costume Designer: Catherine George
Principal Cast: Shirley Henderson (Joy), Michael Kenneth Williams (Allen), Allison Janney (Trish), Michael Lerner (Harvey), Dylan Riley Snyder (Timmy), Ciarán Hinds (Bill), Paul Reubens (Andy), Charlotte Rampling (Jacqueline), Ally Sheedy (Helen), Rich Pecci (Mark), Chris Marquette (Billy)
Format: Rawcode RAW, color
98 min.

The Jordan sisters (from *Happiness*) are ten years older. Joy is married to the sex caller Allen, and when she discovers that he cannot quit his habit, she takes off south to visit her mother and sister Trish in Florida, but finds no solace with them, or with Helen, who has cut off all contact with the rest of the clan. Instead, she is visited by the ghosts of Andy and (after he kills himself) Allen as well. Meanwhile, Bill Maplewood is released from prison and goes on a quest to find his son, Billy (now in Oregon), to see whether he has any of his father's sexual proclivities. Trish falls in love with Harvey Wiener (from *Welcome to the Dollhouse*) as her middle child, Timmy, prepares for his bar mitzvah. Timmy's belated discovery of his father's sins sets off a train of consequences.

Dark Horse (2011)
USA
Production: Double Hope Films
Distribution: Virgil Films & Entertainment
Producers: Juan Basanta, Ted Hope, Derrick Tseng
Director: Todd Solondz
Writer: Todd Solondz
Cinematographer: Andrij Parekh
Editor: Kevin Messman
Production Designer: Alex DiGerlando
Art Direction: Dawn Masi
Costume Designer: Kurt and Bart
Principal Cast: Jordan Gelber (Abe), Selma Blair (Miranda, formerly "Vi"),
    Mia Farrow (Phyllis), Christopher Walken (Jackie), Zachary Booth (Justin),
    Donna Murphy (Marie), Tyler Maynard (Jiminy), Justin Bartha (Richard),
    Aasif Mandvi (Mahmoud), Mary Joy (Lori), Peter McRobbie (Arnie)
Format: Digital, color
86 min.
Abe Wertheimer lives at home with his parents. His father is also his boss
    at work in the family real estate development company, and Abe is
    constantly aggravated by his position, yet he does nothing to change it.
    He falls for a woman he meets at a wedding and pursues her with dogged
    determination, despite her being out of his league. She succumbs out of
    her own desperation (she, too, lives at home, and her writing career is
    going nowhere), but leaves it until too late to tell Abe about her hepatitis
    B condition. Finally blowing up at work, Abe has a terrible car accident
    when he pulls out into traffic, losing both his legs. As he rapidly dies of
    complications arising from his contracted hep B, his fiancée falls pregnant
    to his successful doctor brother. Wistfully, his office friend Marie dreams of
    what might have been after the funeral.

Wiener-Dog (2016)
USA
Production: Annapurna Pictures
Distribution: IFC Films
Producers: Megan Ellison, Christine Vachon
Director: Todd Solondz
Writer: Todd Solondz
Cinematographer: Edward Lachman
Editor: Kevin Messman
Composer: Nathan Larson, James Lavino
Production Designer: Akin McKenzie
Art Direction: Max Wixom

Costume Designer: Amela Baksic

Principal Cast: Keaton Nigel Cooke (Remi), Tracy Letts (Danny), Julie Delpy (Dina), Greta Gerwig (Dawn Wiener), Kieran Culkin (Brandon), Rigoberto Garcia (José), Connor Long (Tommy), Bridget Brown (April), Charlie Tahan (Warren), Danny DeVito (Dave Schmerz), Devin Druid (Dwight), Sharon Washington (Phillips), Andrew Pang (Tseng), Samrat Chakrabarti (Dr. Farhard Rahman), Anna Baryshnikov (Tara), Ari Gaynor (Carol Steinhart), Kett Turton (Director), Ellen Burstyn (Nana), Marcella Lowery (Yvette), Zosia Mamet (Zoe), Michael James Shaw (Fantasy), Melo Ludwig (Young Nana)

Format: Digital (Digital Cinema Package DCP), color

88 min.

A four-part film. In the first, young Remi, a cancer survivor, is given a dachshund by his father. The dog has to be spayed, and when it returns from the vet, it starts defecating and bleeding everywhere, and the parents return it. In the second part, Dawn Wiener rescues the dog from being destroyed at the vet, and they go on a road trip together with Brandon to his brother's home, where he conveys the news of their father's death. There is an Intermission, featuring a song about the legend of the wiener-dog. The third part finds the dog in New York City, cared for by a disappointed screenwriter who teaches at a college. As he realizes his career is over, the screenwriter straps a bomb to the dog and lets it loose in the building, where it is safely captured and decommissioned. The last part concerns the aging Nana, who has renamed the dog "Cancer." Her granddaughter visits for lunch and brings her new boyfriend, a hip young artist. Nana signs her a blank check and then goes outside, where she is visited by nine apparitions of herself as a child. The dog is run over and finally appears mounted as a taxidermy installation piece in an art gallery.

Bibliography

Berlant, Lauren. "A Properly Political Concept of Love: Three Approaches in Ten Pages." *Cultural Anthropology* 26, no. 4 (2011): 683–91.

Breckon, Anna. "Being Unlikeable: The Failure and Optimism of Todd Solondz." *Screen* 59, no. 3 (2018): 311–32.

Brooks, Xan. "Todd Solondz's Pursuit of Happiness." *The Guardian*, September 11, 2009. https://www.theguardian.com/film/2009/sep/10/todd-solondz-life-during-wartime.

Davies, Jon. "Imagining Intergenerationality: Representation and Rhetoric in the Pedophile Movie." *GLQ: A Journal of Lesbian and Gay Studies* 13, no. 2 (2007): 369–85.

DeFino, Dean. "Todd Solondz." In *Fifty Contemporary Film Directors*, 2nd ed., edited by Yvonne Tasker. Routledge Key Guides (London: Routledge, 2011), 369.

Hindes, Andrew. "Letter from Hollywood: How Happiness Won." *The Independent* (UK), October 25, 1998, 16.

Lachman, Ed. "On *Life During Wartime*." Criterion commentary on *Life During Wartime*, Criterion Collection #574 (New York: 2011).

"Life During Wartime: Interview with Todd Solondz." *Electric Sheep: A Deviant View of Cinema*, April 5, 2010. http://www.electricsheepmagazine.co.uk/features/2010/04/05/life-during-wartime-interview-with-todd-solondz.

Mottram, James. "Why Is Director Todd Solondz Returning to the Film That Nearly Destroyed His Career?" *The Independent* (UK), March 28, 2010. https://www.independent.co.uk/arts-entertainment/films/features/why-is-director-todd-solondz-returning-to-the-film-that-nearly-destroyed-his-career-1926742.html.

Murphy, J. J. "Life During Wartime." *j. j. murphy on independent cinema.* http://www.jjmurphyfilm.com/blog/2010/09/17/life-during-wartime.

Newman, Michael Z. "Indie Culture: In Pursuit of the Authentic Autonomous Alternative." *Cinema Journal* 48, no. 3 (2009): 16–34.

Raymond, Marc. "Too Smart, Too Soon: The King of Comedy and American Independent Cinema." *Film Criticism* 34, no. 1 (2009): 17–35, 92.

"Round Table: Independence in the Cinema." *October* 91 (Winter 2000): 3–23.

Sconce, Jeffrey. "Irony, Nihilism, and the New American 'Smart' Film." *Screen* 43, no. 4 (2002): 349–69.

Smith, Paul. "Uneasy Dreams." *Film Quarterly* 63, no. 2 (2009/10): 52–53.

Vachon, Christine. *Shooting to Kill: How an Independent Producer Blasts through the Barriers to Make Movies That Matter.* New York: Quill, 2002.

Walters, Ben. "Todd Only Knows." *Sight & Sound* 20, no. 5 (2010): 8, 2.

Weiner, Jonah. "Solondz Nurtures His Indie Cred." *New York Times*, July 16, 2010. http://www.nytimes.com/2010/07/18/movies/18solodnz.html.

Videos and Podcasts

"In Conversation with Todd Solondz." https://www.youtube.com/watch?v=6ffj5XiWWjI.

"Life During Wartime: Interview with Todd Solondz." KQED Arts (August 5, 2010). https://www.kqed.org/arts/31536/life_during_wartime_interview_with_todd_solondz.

"Todd Solondz on Independent Film." https://www.youtube.com/watch?v=UNpIPar52cA.

"Todd Solondz and Paul Reubens on *Life During Wartime*." *Off-Ramp*, 84.3 KPCC Radio. http://www.scpr.org/programs/offramp/2010/07/31/15703/todd-solondz-and-paul-reubens-on-life-during-warti.

"WTF Podcast with Todd Solondz." https://www.youtube.com/watch?v=EKm7PE5bSZM.

Index

2046 (Wong), 58

Adams, Jane, 17, 60, 62, 95
Adorno, Theodor W., 125, 126
Air Supply, 125–26
Allen, Woody, 27, 130
All That Heaven Allows (Sirk), 45
Altman, Robert, 26
amor fati, 53, 64, 85
Anderson, Paul Thomas, 116
Anderson, Perry, 128
Anger, Kenneth, 27
Augé, Marc, 10

Baker, Dylan, 69, 94
Balzac, Honoré de, 57, 58, 139
Barkin, Ellen, 50
Barthes, Roland, 63
Benjamin, Walter, 39–40
Bergman, Ingmar, 142
Bergson, Henri, 84
Berlant, Lauren, 38
Blair, Selma, 14, 56
Bolter, Jay David, 36
Bradshaw, Peter, 67
Brando, Marlon, 48
Brecht, Bertolt, 49
Buñuel, Luis, 97
Burstyn, Ellen, 93, 101

capitalism: anal, 118–23; art under, 127–28, 131, 161; circulation and, 5, 115, 118, 119, 131; class struggle, 24–25; consumer, 121–26, 156; exploitation of

labour, 23–25; falling rate of profit, 4–6, 119, 130
Cassavetes, John, 27, 35
character, 63–65
China, 83–84
Chopin, 28, 29, 126
cinema, profitability of, 5–6
Citizen Kane (Welles), 130
Civilization and Its Discontents (Freud), 110
Clark, Larry, 35
classicism, 7, 28, 34–40, 44, 46, 51–52, 73, 93, 97, 124, 129, 131
Clover, Joshua, 131
Coppola, Francis Ford, 48
Coppola, Sophia, 26

Dark Horse, 12–17, 39, 50, 53–55, 86, 96, 98–100, 122, 124, 151, 155–56
Debussy, Claude, 108, 109, 155
Deleuze, Gilles, 84–85
Deren, Maya, 27
drive, the, 17, 40, 64, 83–87, 90
Dr. Strangelove (Kubrick), 49

ejaculate, 115–17
Eliot, George, 84
Eliot, T. S., 34–35
eternal recurrence, 52–54
excrement, 21, 88–89, 107–31, 158

Faber, Matthew, 82
fantasy, 92–103
Farocki, Harun, 118–19

Faulkner, William, 57, 58, 139
Fear, Anxiety, and Depression, 27–28, 37
Florida, 12, 57, 60, 69, 70, 78, 81
Freud, Sigmund, 9, 66, 70, 90, 110–11

Gelber, Jordan, 12, 134n36, 143
Giamatti, Paul, 22, 160
Godard, Jean-Luc, 118–19
Godfather trilogy, 47, 48
Goldwyn, Samuel, 157
Greenberg, Clement, 125, 126
Greimas, A. J., 35–36
Grieg, Edvard, 30
Groundhog Day (Ramis), 129
Grusin, Richard, 36
Guinness, Alec, 49
Gursky, Andreas, 151

Happiness, 8, 9, 17–18, 28, 39, 57–68, 73, 76, 77, 86, 94–96, 102–4, 112–22, 125, 128–31, 159–60
Haynes, Todd, 26, 35, 49, 121, 140, 151
Henderson, Shirley, 12, 62, 65, 70
Hinds, Ciarán, 17, 65, 69–70
Hirst, Damien, 127
Hitchcock, Alfred, 115, 117
Hoffman, Philip Seymour, 62, 70, 103
Hollywood, 6, 7, 27, 35–37, 39, 40, 48, 91, 120, 130, 158, 162
Hulk, The (Lee), 48
humanism, 8

I'm Not There (Haynes), 26, 49, 140, 151–52
In the Mood for Love (Wong), 58
Israel, 77–80

Jarmusch, Jim, 35, 36
junkspace, 9–12

Kind Hearts and Coronets (Hamer), 49
kitsch, 124–26, 161–62
Koolhaas, Rem, 9
Korine, Harmony, 35, 36
Kubrick, Stanley, 105
Kuchar, George, 27
Kuchar, Mike, 36

Lacan, Jacques, 111
Lachman, Ed, 26, 59–60, 146
Larson, Nathan, 42, 43, 71, 155
Laughton, Charles, 44, 45
Lee, Spike, 27
Lefebvre, Henri, 9
Leigh, Jennifer Jason, 47, 50
Lewis, Herschell Gordon, 36
Life During Wartime, 12, 17, 26, 57–86, 100–101, 123, 151
Linklater, Richard, 35, 36, 140
Lola Montès (Ophuls), 45
Long takes, 103–9, 153–54
Lost Highway (Lynch), 49
Lovitz, Jon, 17, 62
Lynch, David, 35, 49, 58, 146

Magnolia (1999), 116
Marx, Karl, 25, 84, 131
Matarazzo, Heather, 28, 50
melancholia, 15, 19, 20, 45, 53, 66–67, 71, 78, 132
Mendes, Sam, 140–41
Molière, 39–40
Moonfleet (Lang), 45
Moonlight (Jenkins), 48
Mozart, 73, 145
multiple actors in a role, 46–51

Nealon, Christopher, 131
New Jersey, 20, 54, 57, 72, 118
Nietzsche, Friedrich, 52–53, 64, 85
Night and Fog (Resnais), 45
Night of the Hunter, The (Laughton), 44, 45, 149

O'Brien, Conan, 96
Ordet (1955), 45

Palindromes, 1, 19–20, 38–39, 40–52, 53, 65, 81–83, 86, 87, 102, 105–6, 124, 126, 147–49, 155
Paradjanov, Sergei, 102
Pather Panchali (Ray), 45
Psycho (Hitchcock), 115

Ray, Satyajit, 45, 48

Reubens, Paul, 65, 70
Roberts, Michael, 4
romanticism, 34–35

satire, 3, 6–8, 22, 42, 61, 68–69, 80, 93, 97, 100, 103, 109, 124, 127, 131, 157, 159, 160
Sayles, John, 35, 36
Schamus, James, 121–22
Sconce, Jeffrey, 35, 36
Sellers, Peter, 49
sequels, 64–66, 78, 82
Sexton III, Brendan, 29, 90
Shining, The (Kubrick), 106
Silverman, Kaja, 118–19
Sitcom, 20, 58, 129, 146
Smiles of a Summer Night (Bergman), 45
Soderbergh, Steven, 26
Solondz, Todd: "restrained simplicity" of, 26–27, 40, 46, 124; artists in the work of, 127–28, 160; classicism of, 29–41, 44, 46, 51–52, 73, 124; *Dark Horse*, 12–17, 39, 50, 53–55, 86, 96, 98–100, 122, 124, 151, 155–56; digital technology and, 153; directors of photography and, 146; editors of, 152; *Fear, Anxiety, and Depression*, 27–28, 37; *Happiness*, 8, 9, 17–18, 28, 39, 57–68, 73, 76, 77, 86, 94–96, 102–4, 112–22, 125, 128–31, 159–60; *Life During Wartime*, 12, 17, 26, 57–86, 100–101, 123, 151; music in the works of, 155–56; *Palindromes*, 1, 19–20, 38–39, 40–52, 53, 65, 81–83, 86, 87, 102, 105–6, 124, 126, 147–49, 155; *Storytelling*, 20–25, 56, 96–97, 104, 122, 124, 126–27, 144–45; *Welcome to the Dollhouse*, 1, 6, 9, 28–34, 36–37, 64, 81, 83, 86–90, 93–94, 111–12, 124, 126, 130; *Wiener-Dog*, 8, 10–12, 18–19, 26, 37, 55, 68, 86, 87–93, 101–3, 107–9, 119, 131–32, 148, 150

Sound of Music, The (Wise), 45, 140, 147
South Park, 119
Star Wars (Lucas), 6, 47–48, 58, 139
Storytelling, 20–25, 56, 96–97, 104, 122, 124, 126–27, 144–45
Swift, Jonathan, 7

Tarkovsky, Andrei, 102
telephone, 118
television, 20–21, 43, 58, 61, 128–31, 146–47
Toys"R"Us, 12–13, 54–55, 99, 123, 151
Twin Peaks: Fire Walk with Me (Lynch), 58

value, cinema and, 6, 65, 118–19, 131–32
Van Sant, Gus, 36
Vigo, Jean, 108, 154
Von Trier, Lars, 41, 151

Walken, Christopher, 14, 143
Walker, Christine, 65
Warhol, Andy, 27
Waters, John, 27, 36
Webber, Mark, 50
Weekend (Godard), 118, 154
Welcome to the Dollhouse, 1, 6, 9, 28–34, 36–37, 64, 81, 83, 86–90, 93–94, 111–12, 124, 126, 130
Welles, Orson, 35, 130
Wiener-Dog, 8, 10–12, 18–19, 26, 37, 55, 68, 86, 87–93, 101–3, 107–9, 119, 131–32, 148, 150
Williams, Michael Kenneth, 62, 65, 70
Wong Kar-Wai, 58

Zarathustra, 52
Zéro de conduite (Vigo), 108
Žižek, Slavoj, 123

Index | 175

Julian Murphet is Scientia Professor in film and literature in the School of the Arts and Media at the University of New South Wales. His books include *Faulkner's Media Romance* and *Multimedia Modernism: Literature and the Anglo-American Avant-garde*.

Books in the series Contemporary Film Directors

Nelson Pereira dos Santos
Darlene J. Sadlier

Abbas Kiarostami
Mehrnaz Saeed-Vafa and Jonathan Rosenbaum

Joel and Ethan Coen
R. Barton Palmer

Claire Denis
Judith Mayne

Wong Kar-wai
Peter Brunette

Edward Yang
John Anderson

Pedro Almodóvar
Marvin D'Lugo

Chris Marker
Nora Alter

Abel Ferrara
Nicole Brenez, translated by Adrian Martin

Jane Campion
Kathleen McHugh

Jim Jarmusch
Juan Suárez

Roman Polanski
James Morrison

Manoel de Oliveira
John Randal Johnson

Neil Jordan
Maria Pramaggiore

Paul Schrader
George Kouvaros

Jean-Pierre Jeunet
Elizabeth Ezra

Terrence Malick
Lloyd Michaels

Sally Potter
Catherine Fowler

Atom Egoyan
Emma Wilson

Albert Maysles
Joe McElhaney

Jerry Lewis
Chris Fujiwara

Jean-Pierre and Luc Dardenne
Joseph Mai
Michael Haneke
Peter Brunette

Alejandro González Iñárritu
Celestino Deleyto and Maria del Mar Azcona

Lars von Trier
Linda Badley

Hal Hartley
Mark L. Berrettini

François Ozon
Thibaut Schilt

Steven Soderbergh
Aaron Baker

Mike Leigh
Sean O'Sullivan

D.A. Pennebaker
Keith Beattie

Jacques Rivette
Mary M. Wiles

Kim Ki-duk
Hye Seung Chung

Philip Kaufman
Annette Insdorf

Richard Linklater
David T. Johnson

David Lynch
Justus Nieland

John Sayles
David R. Shumway

Dario Argento
L. Andrew Cooper

Todd Haynes
Rob White

Christian Petzold
Jaimey Fisher

Spike Lee
Todd McGowan

Terence Davies
Michael Koresky

Francis Ford Coppola
Jeff Menne

Emir Kusturica
Giorgio Bertellini

Agnès Varda
Kelley Conway

John Lasseter
Richard Neupert

Paul Thomas Anderson
George Toles

Cristi Puiu
Monica Filimon

Wes Anderson
Donna Kornhaber

Jan Švankmajer
Keith Leslie Johnson

Kelly Reichardt
Katherine Fusco and Nicole Seymour

Michael Bay
Lutz Koepnick

Abbas Kiarostami, Expanded Second Edition
Mehrnaz Saeed-Vafa and Jonathan Rosenbaum

Lana and Lilly Wachowski
Cáel M. Keegan

Todd Solondz
Julian Murphet

The University of Illinois Press
is a founding member of the
Association of University Presses.

University of Illinois Press
1325 South Oak Street
Champaign, IL 61820-6903
www.press.uillinois.edu